Rags to Riches

The Horses That Made Racing Pay

John Budden

FRONT COVER; left to right, Mister Baileys goes to post before winning the 2,000 Guineas; Flakey Dove inspects a hurdle; Lochsong beats Paris House at York.

FRONT COVER SILHOUETTE; Jodami with Peter Beamont and Anthea Farrell

BACK COVER; Jodami leaps a fence.

THE AUTHOR

John Budden was born in 1939 and lives in Cumbria. He is a well known journalist and commentator, especially in the North. As well as writing a regular column in The Sporting Life and for Pacemaker, he writes under "Borderer" in the Racing and Football Outlook, and as "Pat Lane" in the Weekly News. He also writes for the Cumberland News, and is Border T V's racing expert. More recently he has worked as a commentator for Racecall and he has been an established race course commentator in the North for more years than he cares to remember. His dulcet tones are often heard in betting shops via S. I. S. coverage. In his spare time he plays golf and cricket.

Copyright ©PRIDE OF PLACE PUBLISHING

This Edition First published in 1994
by
Pride of Place Publishing

10 9 8 7 6 5 4 3 2 1

British Library Cataloguing in Publication Data.
A catalogue record for this book is available from
the British Library.

ISBN 1-874645-06-X

Typeset by
READ THIS PUBLISHING,

Printed in Great Britain by BPC Wheatons Ltd, Exeter

PRIDE OF PLACE PUBLISHING LTD
UNIT 9, CBTC,
EUXTON LANE, CHORLEY
LANCASHIRE, PR7 6TE

CONTENTS

FOREWORD

'Rags to Riches' is a much misunderstood phrase. After all poverty and wealth are comparative labels.

Several of my friends plead poverty when one knows from the cars in which they travel to the racecourse that they are not all that short.

Others exude prosperity in public but in private can hardly bear to open their monthly bank statements.

To some all the sixteen horses listed here will have cost a fortune. A few would indeed seem to have required serious money.

The choice though is personal and their inclusion has been based on the proportion of prize money earnt in relation to original purchase price.

John Budden, March 1994

FOREST KING

This is the blueprint for all bargains. The winner who cost peaanuts and so nearly started favourite for the Grand National in his first season over fences. Shades of Elizabeth Taylor and National Velvet all over again. Come to think of it Forest King and Velvet had plenty in common but I fear that it was easier for Miss Taylor to impersonate an inexperienced teenage 'conditional' than it would be for Ron Barry to pass himself off as the delectable young child actress! Mind you Forest King wasn't Irish. He was Cumbrian born and bred and Ken Hogg his ebullient owner trainer was born near Appleby, the county town of Westmorland and lived anyhow for the duration of Forest King's active career in the village of Yanwath, less than 5 miles from the centre of Penrith. 'Hoggy' has been an entrepreneur and a 'go getter' all his life. His father was a livestock dealer but Ken was as far removed from the image of the dour Cumbrian farmer as Ian Botham is from Geoff Boycott.

Charisma is his middle name - after the glory days of Forest King, he emerged as a highly successful night club owner. His son continues to run Rookin House, the riding school and trekking centre at Troutbeck where Forest King built up his stamina carrying his substantially built owner up the steep fellside tracks.

A brush with the constabulary over alleged late night drinking at his "Glendowlen" night club in 1982 led to Ken Hogg selling up and emigrating - he spent nine months living rough with the last genuine cowboys in Texas, and a further three years commuting between Scandinavia and France, specialising in 'Trotters'. Before settling in the Isle of Man he was involved in an ambitious plan to buy thoroughbreds in England export them to Spain and prepare them to race at the new track that the Spanish authorities were proposing to create at Estapona near Marbella.

The racecourse never got past the drawing board but Ken escaped without burning his fingers.

He now trains a string of horses for the White family at Ballagarrow and regularly raids the northern courses with the like of Kinoko and Top Show.

His methods have never been orthodox but working with horses has been an integral part of Ken's life.

Well before the arrival of Forest King, he was "dealing" with the gypsies at the annual Appleby Horse Fair and there is still a touch of the Romany about his approach to training. First and foremost he seeks to influence the horse's "psyche"; to strike a common bond that will result in horse and trainer working in unison.

"Hoggy" has always engaged in this "one to one" relationship with his horses and none more so than with Forest King, the inspiration behind his training career.

Neighbouring farmer Ken Tuer liked his racing. He kept a modest brood mare called Workington Wanderer who had run without success as a two year old but had already produced a gutsy hurdler called Cool Angel, who Tuer sold to

Hughie Redbanks, a close friend who farmed at Shap.

Forest King was the mare's second foal and later she was to produce further winners in Cool Imp and Cool Gabriel. All four were sired by Rubor, who stood at Jack Williams' Lynsted Stud at High Hesket..

There was something about Forest King that appealed to Ken Hogg. Later he was to admit that the horse had always given him a special buzz. To me, Forest King had been an Arkle from the moment that I first set eyes on him as a foal and when I got the offer to buy him, I jumped at the chance!

The deal was struck "over a jar or two" after returning from Penrith market. Tuer accepted £125 in readies and Forest King got a lift down in the cattle truck.

His formative years were spent at Troutbeck, assisting with the trekking and occasionally acting as his owner's hack. He was no oil painting; in fact later commentators were charitable when they described him as "tough, workmanlike and plain".

He was certainly tough and my own abiding memory of Forest King concerns the size of his feet. To extend the cricketing simile they were the equine version of Curtley Ambrose's size fourteens.

They may have been huge but they were to operate with remarkable efficiency when the ground rode heavy.

By the time that Forest King had turned four, his elder brother Cool Angel had already won several races over hurdles and encouraged by both Redbanks and Tuer, Ken began to gallop his powerhouse in earnest.

The trials were surprisingly promising. Forest King revealed an unexpected turn of foot and unlimited resources of stamina.

"I decided there and then to have a go" recalls Hogg. "I put by a few hundred pounds to finance the venture and set my sights on running him over hurdles in the Autumn of 1974".

Ken had first to persuade the Jockey Club to grant him a permit. In those less stringent days this didn't present a serious problem..

Raymond Titterington, who trained a small string at Skelton near Penrith, and Lord Inglewood from Hutton In The Forest acted as referees and the relevant papers from Portman Square were soon winging their way northwards.

Forest King was put through his paces and by the time he was declared for Kelso in November expectations were high.

"What we didn't know, was that Frank Carr had a rod in pickle called Pottersville", remembers Ken. Our fellow ran a brave race but Pottersville had been backed down to 4/5 and was never really in danger of being caught".

The young amateur who partnered Forest King in his early races was Kevin Gray and among the other members of his unpaid ranks involved in that first race were both Ridley Lamb and Johnnie Bradburne.

'Hoggy' and his partners recouped their losses at Leicester where Forest King started at 8/13 and won comfortably by 6 lengths from So Ray, the mount of Paul Felgate.

He was to win four more races that season before venturing south to run a creditable fifth in The George Duller Hurdle at Cheltenham's April meeting, one place ahead of Ron Barry on Ribanco.

'Big Ron' was impressed and volunteered his services both as jockey and gallops consultant. His advice was invaluable and 'Hoggy' gained tremendous pleasure from training his pride and joy.

"He was right for me" explains Ken. "The horse had bags of personality and I was able to bring that out. I've never known a tougher horse".

Just how resilient he was can be seen from his schedule for the early months of 1976.

Forest King and Ron Barry had already won five chases by mid-January; at which point the rider advised a rest but Ken did not agree. He told Ron that in his opinion the horse was "very happy in himself" and that he intended to go on running him for as long as he remained keen.

His next outing came on January 28th, Forest King partnered by Barry won the Cumberland Grand National Trial by an easy 4 lengths from Meridian II despite carrying the steadier of 12st 3lbs. A week later the combination landed the Dipper Chase at Newcastle.

His tally was now seven wins from ten outings. Ron demanded that the horse should be given a rest. It was not to be.

Ken Hogg announced his intention of running his horse in the Haydock Park National Trial the following Wednesday and if successful aiming him for the gruelling 4 mile Eider Chase at Newcastle - four demanding races within the space of little more than 3 weeks. Ron Barry gave vent to his feelings and was replaced by David Munro.

The substitute jockey duly completed the Haydock Park-Eider Chase double and Munro retained the ride for the Sun Alliance Novices Chase, Forest King's thirteenth race of the season.

He started 3/1 second favourite and never got further than the second fence. Ken remembers the disaster clearly. "There was such a lot of bunching approaching the fence and Forest King was hopelessly unsighted. He ran straight into the belly of the birch and catapulted David Munro out of the saddle".

Unpeturbed by this set back 'Hoggy' now planned to saddle Forest King in the Grand National.

Chris Mordaunt handicapped him among the top weights on 11st 11bs but the punters were not deterred.

A week before the big race he was antepost favourite and his devoted owner-trainer had already rejected an offer of 23 grand.

"With hindsight I was naive" continues Ken. "Thousands of pounds in bets were riding on his back but apart from buying a guard dog, I did not take any serious precautions. Forest King was nobbled. There can't be any doubt about that and Noel, the bookmaker from nearby Penrith was equally convinced that "The Needle Man" had done his job".

Ken explains, "Noel had said to me only the previous week that it would cost him 12 grand if Forest King were to win the National. Now Noel never did an evil thing in his whole life but if he stood to lose that sort of money other buggers more unscupulous than Noel would have had liabilities ten times as large. I'm sure Forest King was got at and there are guys living today who know exactly what happened to him that Friday night".

Ken had arranged to give Forest King his final fast bit of work at Newcastle racecourse the Saturday before Aintree.

He continues - "Kingy was a little lame when he walked out of the wagon. He'd been absolutely bouncing at home. I'd never had him better and to start with I didn't think it was much. The gallop went ahead and I decided to call the vet from home".

The workout proved an anti climax. The saddle slipped and by the time Ken and Forest King reached Cumbria the leg was bad. The vet diagnosed tendon trouble but Hogg was not happy with the diagnosis. By Sunday night the leg was swollen solid from top to bottom.

"Even his eyes were beginning to glass over", recalls Ken. "I couldn't believe it. 48 hours earlier the horse had been on top of the world and here he was almost dropping in front of me."

Forest King was scratched from the National and did not reappear that season.

"I was certain that the horse hadn't damaged a tendon" said Hogg "but it wasn't until I was talking about the mystery to some top vets in Newmarket two years afterwards that the truth emerged.

Forest King had been injected with a dose of Copper Sulphate and the only possible antidote would have been immediate treatment with Penicillin".

Forest King continued to enjoy his tankard of Guinness and tour the Lake District tracks but as a power on the course, he was never quite the same.

He won only once from 12 outings in 1976 to 1977 and finished out of the money in the National. Critics blamed the Cumbrian Permit Holder for taking him to the well" too many times as a six year old but Ken Hogg knows otherwise. The gelding regained a fraction of his earlier sparkle the following season when he scored at Newcastle and was trained specifically for Aintree.

Ron Barry, back in the saddle and restored to his position as "chief consultant" detected all the old fighting spirit in the run up to the National and the ante post market reflected growing confidence. Ken Hogg himself was buoyant but 24 hours before the race Forest King developed a corn and was withdrawn. A dejected Ron Barry was forced to sit out the race and watch Lucius, the horse he had been asked to ride, triumph in the hands of Bob Davies.

Forest King gained his seventeenth and final success in the Greenall Whitley Red Rum Chase at his favourite Carlisle in September 1978. He finished alone in a field of three, with Ron Barry on board.

'Kingy' made token appearances over the next three seasons before dropping quietly out of the game in 1982.

Forest King spent a long and happy retirement at the home of an old friend who lived in the Fellside village of Melmerby. He cut quite a dash at local fetes and was still hale and hearty at the age of 23 when he was reclaimed by Ken Hogg to spend the remainder of his days at Ballagarrow.

"But for a freak accident Forest King would be alive today" says an emotional Ken. "He was out at grass in his paddock when one of his compatriots lashed out and kicked him directly on the shin. His leg was broken and despite titanic efforts by all concerned we couldn't save him. It was the saddest day of my life".

Forest King cost £125. He won 17 races and netted nearly £20,000 in winning prize money - a great deal of cash in the mid-seventies when the level of returns can be gauged from the figure that Ken Hogg received after Forest King won his first race at Leicester. First prize amounted to £204!

KEY TO MY HEART

Dudley Moffatt knows a bargain. He has the make and build of a jockey and has spent the greater part of his life among horses; in Cheshire with Eric Cousins, in Northumberland with George Fairbairn and more recently with Roger Fisher at Ulverston.

Since 1984 he has trained a small but successful string at Pit Farm Racing Stables little more than a stone's throw away from the starting gate at Cartmel.

Few of his winners have cost a five figure sum and Key To My Heart is a typical Moffatt purchase.

The trainer bought him for 5000 guineas at the Doncaster sales and was pleased with the buy. Dudley is no mind reader however and had he realised that after only two seasons in training Key To My Heart would have netted £34,790 in winning prize money he might well have been tempted to keep 'The Colt' in the family!

Dual purpose horses are the flavour of the month at Pit Farm and Dudley had gone to Doncaster with the intention of "getting something that would run on the flat and then go hurdling" - the make of the horse rather than its pedigree is the Cartmel trainer's priority and Key To My Heart's physical appearance was his main attraction.

"He is a beautifully made horse. His conformation is superb

- good legs; a lovely outlook; you know a good honest head!"

A lot of trainers stress the importance of this characteristic and there is no doubting the accuracy of Dudley's description.

Key To My Heart looks at you straight in the eye - direct contact from a noble brow. There's nothing shrewd, laid back or cunning about his gaze. The cut of his jaw as they say is forceful and determined. He looks the sort to be trusted to give of his best whatever the question.

He's also too good to be sent over hurdles - as his trainer says - "I don't think this horse will go over the hurdles - certainly not this year".

5000 guineas is a paltry sum for a horse who is capable of winning in Group 3 company, so why was it that Key To My Heart failed to attract a higher bid?

The answer probably lies in his breeding. Broken Hearted was a first season stallion at the time of the Doncaster sale and the dam's sire Godswalk has had his limitations exposed at stud.

Dudley was pleasantly surprised at the success of his bid. He recalls - "I got him pretty easily. People mistrusted his pedigree but I liked the way he moved and after all Godswalk was classy enough to win the Irish 2000 Guineas".

First impressions are usually the best and Key To My Heart has never given Dudley Moffatt any cause to regret his payment of 5000 guineas.

"He's tough and loves his job" continues the trainer. "He loves to gallop but at the same time he's very sensible with it. You can settle him and switch him off but once you press the button - phiff! he certainly can quicken".

Key To My Heart is owned in partnership by Marjory
Thompson from Kendal and Maureen Pickering whose husband has been in the Licenced Victuallers trade for more
years than he cares to remember. The Pickerings have
recently sold their pub in Barrow and Key To My Heart is the
first horse in which Maureen has had an interest. She is a
frequent visitor to the Moffatt stable and never arrives empty
handed.

"She spoils him" says Dudley. "Always brings a handful of
carrrots and Key To My Heart is partial to that vegetable".

Marjory Thompson in contrast is an experienced horse-
woman. "I've known her since I was a child" says Dudley
with some feeling. Marjory was the principal owner of Bridge
Player and she knows the time of day.

Moffatt trained two year olds often learn their job at
Hamilton on the easy ground early on in the spring. Key To
My Heart was no exception. He made his debut at the
Scottish course in April 1992 and upset both Jack Berry and
the majority of punters by beating the Berry hot pot Sabre
Rattler.

Jack blamed the starter for letting them go when his horse
was facing the wrong way (the starting stalls had got bogged
down in the mud) but I think he was just a bit "rattled"
because the video exonerates everyone at the start.

Key To My Heart went on to win from Finmental at Thirsk
but was then beaten in the Cock of the North stakes at
Doncaster.

"He went a bit weak on us and I rested him for a couple of

months", recalls Dudley. "We brought him back for York's September fixture. He finished third beaten two heads by Devilry and Chevrotain but with due respect to his rider he should have won. Key To My Heart never saw daylight until well inside the final furlong and was flying at the time. The colt subsequently ran with much promise in nurseries."

"As a two year old he was a much better horse than his form suggested", maintains his trainer "This is a very good horse".

Key To My Heart went a long way to justifying this opinion as a three year old. He nearly won first time out at Haydock and was the moral winner of his second race at Chester, though the formbook proves that he was beaten in a photo by League Leader.

"Dean McKeown rang me that night to say he should have won" says Dudley. "He admitted that he got messed about on the home turn and had to come wide".

Kieran Fallon rode the colt for the rest of the season and displayed admirable judgement to win The Foss Stakes at York's July meeting by a length from Top Cees.

On the strength of that performance Key To My Heart was aimed at the Tote Ebor in August. I fancied him to go close at the attractive price and the Sporting Life carried a feature on the colt, the morning of the Ebor. - the piece shared the back page with Life's ace tipster Mark Winstanley of 'Beat the Book' fame. Mark was not so sweet on his chances and did not disguise his feelings. In the event Key To My Heart ran a most creditable race to finish fourth to Sarawat.

The winner was in front a long way from home and Kieran felt obliged to give chase. Still second entering the last furlong, Key To My Heart tied up close home and was passed just short of the line by Oh So Risky and Dreams End.

For a horse whom the critics dismissed as a short runner this was a fair performance and Key To My Heart should arguably have won both his subsequent races..

He went down by half a length to Prince Andros at Doncaster in September and finished third to John Baliol in the Doonside Cup at Ayr's Western meeting, beaten a neck and one length.

Extreme tactics were employed on both occasions . At Town Moor Key To My Heart was surprisingly pulled wide to challenge fully half a mile from the tape. The decision did not meet with the trainer's approval.

"It's a long staring straight at Doncaster", explains Dudley "And young horses do not appreciate being in front for too long. I would have preferred to see him tucked away behind Prince Andros with the intention of coming with a late rattle".

The lesson may have been taken root in Kieran Fallon's mind for in his last race, the Doonside Cup, Key To My Heart was dropped some eight lengths off the pace and could not close with the leaders when the gallop quickened over the last three furlongs. The close up read "Out paced until final furlong; kept on well!".

Key To My Heart had done more than enough.. He was put away for the season but Dudley was far from unhappy.

"He finished off on a good note and was actually a better horse at the end of the season. He'd just come to himself and took his last two races extremely well. Early on he had to have a fortnight between races to recover, doing nothing. In the autumn he was bouncing two days after he'd run".

Key To My Heart remained at Pit Farm all winter. Throughout October and November he was turned out to grass everyday. He never saw a saddle and enjoyed himself cantering quietly around the Moffatt's back paddock.

"We brought him back in about Christmas time and I could see that he'd trained on. He loves to race and is very genuine" said his trainer.

"He's just a cheeky chap in his box, nothing nasty but he'll nibble at your jacket if you don't watch him".

Dudley likes to ride him out most mornings though his eldest son Jimmy is an able deputy.

"Dad thinks I'm a bit too heavy to work him all the time" says Jimmy Moffatt; "But what really frightens him is the thought that I might persuade Key To My Heart to go hurdling instead."

Back in January Dudley was confident that Key To My Heart would win in "listed company".

He did not have to wait long to be proved right. After a preliminary warm up in the John Porter at Newbury the colt took his place in The Group 2 Yorkshire Cup at the May meeting. He led all the way to win at 16/1 in the hands of John Reid. That proven performer My Patriarch was 3½ lengths back in second place.

"They thought it was a fluke", said Dudley "but I knew we'd won fair and square. Mind you I was a bit shocked to see John (Reid) taking him to the front so early. I'd told him to tuck him away!"

Reid had ridden a fine tactical race. Sensing that there was no pace, he'd dictated the gallop from the start and when Key To My Heart quickened "inside the three" the race as good as over.

The colt's next outing was delayed until Newmarket's July meeting. Alan Munro had the mount in the Group 2 Princess of Wales Stakes. Key To My Heart finished fifth to Wagon Master beaten two short heads out of third place.

Dudley Moffatt was furious. "The jockey gave him much too hard a race. I told him to lay up handy and he had him flat out in front from the start", growled the Cartmel trainer.

Despite his exertions on the July course. Key To My Heart reappeared quickly. Dudley explained "He was bouncing within two days and I decided to send him to Ayr for the Tennents Scottish Classic. It was a mistake as things turned out but horses don't talk."

Key To My Heart, ridden by John Carroll improved on to the heels of the leaders turning for home but stopped to nothing within half a furlong. He finished ninth to Beneficial.

"John Carroll sensed that something was badly amiss and eased him right down", recalled Moffatt. "I had him tested and his blood was all wrong".

While he was recuperating connections received a substantial offer for their colt. Kerry Packer, the Australian television mogul, was keen to buy him to run in the Melbourne Cup.

The money was so tempting that for a while it seemed Key To My Heart was on his way to Australia. He passed the vet but the line went suddenly silent. Key To My Heart missed the Greoffrey Freer Stakes at Newbury only to reappear in the Lonsdale Stakes at York.

"He'd missed a lot of work. The ground was too firm and I was delighted that he finished fourth", said Dudley. Key To My Heart has sinced finished a brave second to Dancing Bloom in the Doonside Cup at Ayr's Western Meeting, starting at 9/2 and partnered by Jason Weaver he cruised through to take up the running between the last two furlongs only yo be headed by the favourite close home.

The Australian offer has been scrapped and Key to My Heart stays at Cartmel.

DEBS BALL

Napping winners is meant to be a scientific business. Hours of sweat on the form book helped occasionally by a few encouraging words from connections yields its own rewards. Well that's the idea anyhow but two of my more profitable efforts have resulted more from inspiration than graft. Not a single observer gave Ace of Diamond's the ghost of a chance when he landed a Sedgefield seller at 25/1 and the cupboard was equally bare when Debs Ball was selected as the hopeful selection to win the Grade 2, West Yorkshire Hurdle at Wetherby on the last day of October 1993. The recalcitrant mare, bless her heart, duly achieved the impossible by beating Sweet Duke two lengths with the future Champion Hurdle heroine Flakey Dove, a further twelve lengths adrift in fourth place.

The win, received in subdued manner by the packed crowds at Wetherby but enthusiastically cheered home in "the commentator's crows nest" at faraway Ayr, was the fifteenth and most valuable of Debs Ball's varied career.

There were even a few supreme optimists who held out hopes that Debs Ball would repeat this happy shock in the Bonusprint Stayers hurdle at Cheltenham in March. Sadly they were doomed to disappointment. "Debs" disliked the undulations dropped herself out and had called it a day shortly after halfway.

Not to worry there will be other happier occasions very probably at Netherby in October. The fascination about Debs Ball is her unpredictability; the joy is to select the right race, watch her pick up the bit with a furlong to run, and stand transfixed as she changes into overdrive and remorselessly cuts down her rivals to hit the front in the shadow of the post: no earlier than that or the enigmatic mare will pull herself up with an alacrity that even Little Bay would envy.

Both horses shared that streak of endearing cussedness which could leave their backers frothing at the mouth and their jockeys powerless to take remedial action.

Debs Ball wasn't cheap. 12,000 Irish punts was the asking price but three of her four owners were insurance brokers so they were aware of the risks and prepared to view "acts of God" with a degree of charity.

John Calvert heads a long established insurance business in Barrow. Margaret Faragher, whose house overlooks the racecourse at nearby Cartmel is a partner. Jim Mottram is an insurance broker in Manchester and Graham Mullen, the odd man out, owns a light engineering firm in Disley.

John Calvert had previously owned Priceoflove who had won twice as a two year old and three times over hurdles before developing 'a leg'.

Debs Ball was purchased as a replacement and ironically she was also lame when John and his co-owners travelled to Ireland to 'inspect the goods'.

He recalls, 'Jimmy (Moffatt) was working for Tommy Stack at the time and he had recommended Debs Ball as a filly with a big future. She hadn't been seriously trained but Jimmy was confident about the feel that she had been giving him on the gallops.

Tommy brought her out of her box and blow me, if she wasn't lame. We didn't know how to react at the beginning but Tommy was a real gentleman. He assured us that the filly had been sound the previous day and that she must have trodden on a stone and bruised her foot coming back from the gallops. He said that he would keep her free of charge for a further month and pay the vet's bills himself if we still wanted to go ahead with the deal. There was never any question about that and she's given us tremendous pleasure ever since.

Debs Ball was beaten three necks, a head and half a length on her first appearance at Thirsk. John Williams had the ride next time out when she started at 20/1 for the Knutsford Stakes at Haydock and she finished fifth.

Unbeknown to this simple observer she was fancied to make it third time lucky in a three year old maiden at Catterick on October 20th 1989.

Kieran Fallon had the ride and Debs Ball swung wide off the hometurn before rallying to finish strongly in third place beaten one and a half lengths and a head. I thought Dudley Moffatt would have been delighted but a glance at his dapper figure jumping up and down and gesticulating frantically in the unsaddlng enclosure taught me otherwise. From that moment onwards not a single race has gone by without careful attention being made to the performance of Debs Ball.

Even as a three year old filly she was a striking individual with a touch of temperament. On the way back from Catterick Debs Ball did her best to break out of the box.

"She's a placid traveller normally, explains Dudley." But if there's another horse in the box behaving badly she can create. She'll stand it for a quarter of an hour but then if her companion is still puting on a show she'll join in, determined to go one better."

It's the same at home in her roomy box at Pit Farm, Cartmel and on the gallops overlooking the race course.

Owner John Calvert takes a careful "raincheck" before handling over the Polo mints and rain is the operative word. If it's wet Debs Ball curls up and doesn't want to know. If the sun is out she needs watching.

Dudley admits that he has to be ready for anything. "She's a right little madam behaving as though she's at a rodeo jumping , kicking and squealing but there's nothing vicious about her. She just takes a lot of knowing."

Dudley Moffatt and his eldest son Jimmy are the only two riders to partner Debs Ball on the home gallops and with due respect to Chris Dennis who had the slightly unenviable task of being in the saddle on her first three outings over hurdles, Debs Ball didn't reveal her full potential until Jimmy took over the reins in the spring of 1990.

"Until we put Jimmy on her she;d never jump; desperate she was", remembers Moffatt Senior." I spent a long time schooling the pair of them together. The language was pretty blue but it paid off in the end."

Debs Ball won her first race in Britain, a novice hurdle at Cartmel in May 1990 by 30 lengths with Jimmy Moffatt in the saddle and the trainers son has partnered the mare to all her subsequent ten victories over timber.

The success has come the hard way and there have been occasions when Jimmy has been criticised by those harsh judges, the massed riders in the stands.

"We found out early on that Debs Ball has to be allowed to drop herself out and run her own race", continues Dudley. "When he first rode her, Jimmy came back saying that he'd given her a couple of slaps with the stick and pushed for all that he was worth but the mare wouldn't have any of it. Thank God he didn't abuse her or she could have become a total thief. Jimmy has learnt that he just has to sit and suffer. Mind you he's taken some stick from people who don;t know any better but I always say that if Lester Piggott and Peter Scudamore were both on her back together, they couldn't make her go if she didn't want to !

The mare's best seasons have been the 1991 Flat Campaign and the 1991-92 National Hunt season. During this period Debs Ball clocked up no less than eight wins, all of them "hand over heart" affairs with connections holding their breath and waiting for her to make her familiar charge from the rear.

"Sometimes even the commentator gets it wrong", remembers John Calvert . "When Debs went in at Catterick's March meeting a year ago, the commentator announced that she was tailed off and out of the race. the next moment, there she was grabbing hold of the bit and passing horse after horse until getting her head in front with about thirty yards to go. It's uncanny how she seems to know exactly where the winning post is!"

At Bangor a couple of season's ago Debs Ball finally won a race without either the commentator or the owner realising that she had done so.

" I was in the office at Barrow. listening to the race on the telephone and put the receiver down when the first three were called passing the post with Debs not among them," relates John Calvert . "Then a minute later my secretary burst into the office with the happy news that the commentator had mistaken the colours and that she'd won after all!"

Last November both owners and trainer astonished their neighbours in the grandstand at Wetherby by shouting at their jockey "to stay where he was and not to get any closer to the leaders." Bearing in mind that the main bulk of the field had already reached the last flight the advice seemed tantamount to contravening that sacred rule about "not putting a horse into the race."

In fact the words were only marginally short of the mark. Debs Ball had gone to the front unusually early and in the normal course of events would have been tempted to down tools on the run to the line. Happily Jimmy Moffatt had judged the situation to a nicety and the mare ran out a comfortable winner from Sweet Duke.

Debs Ball has long captured the imagination of the people of Barrow in Furness. "They always back her", says John Calvert " and don't take a blind bit of notice of the form book. Two days before Cheltenham, the local paper ran a banner headline "Calvert hopes for a Cheltenham Ball", when she tailed herself off by halfway, I didn't think I'd dare show my face in the town again but I needn't have worried; the mare's got such a fan club that their only worry was whether she had come back to Cartmel in one piece".

Debs Ball did just that. As Dudley Moffatt reflects. "She's never had a really hard race because she's doing nothing except idling along in her own time until she decides to accelerate and that will only be over the final quarter of a mile".

Debs Ball has little experience of jumping fences. She tried tackling the major obstables at Doncaster fifteen months ago but got no further than the seventh.

"She jumped the first five perfectly", relates Dudley. "Then she must have thought the whole idea was a piece of cake because she ran right into the bottom of the sixth and never took off at the next which was an open ditch. Poor Jimmy had no chance of staying int the saddle."

The experience persuaded connections to restrict Debs Ball to hurdling and running on the flat.

This sensible decision means that the Cartmel trained mare will be with us for at least until the end of 1994-95. "When she's ten we might suggest to the owners that she retires to the paddocks", says Dudley Moffatt. "She should make a grand broodmare in time".

Debs Ball has been busy for much of the spring and summer of 1994. The mare was more than a shade unlucky in the Petros Long Distance Hurdle at Haydock on May Bank Holiday. She was launching a dangerous looking challenge at the second last flight, only to sprawl left handed through the hurdle and lose all impetus.

Debs Ball finished third to Avro Anson but the stewards ruled that she had interfered with the runner up Sweet Glow. They disqualified Debs Ball and placed her last. Jimmy Moffatt was suspended "for causing intentional interference."

The mare's summer campaign on the level began with two promising runs at Catterick. More recently she finished a fair second to Royal Circus at Hamilton.

Sadly there were no opportunities for her to resume her hurdling career at Cartmel's August meeting but Dudley Moffatt is hoping that she will be in peak form for Wetherby's late

October meeting, when she will attempt to win the West Yorkshire Hurdle for the second consecutive year.

Debs Ball goes on most sorts of ground but she has notoriously thin-soled feet and is prone to bruising her pedal bone on a firm surface.

The mare has won four times on the flat and eleven times over hurdles, winning over £70,000 in prize money.

(NB: since going to print Messrs. Calvert, Mottram and Mullen have dropped out of ownership. Debs Ball is now owned in partnership by Margaret Faraghar, Dudley Moffatt, Eileen Milligan and Brian Clark, a Cumbrian farmer).

BLYTON LAD

"The letters to the editor" column in both of racing's "trade papers" makes compulsory reading. Correspondents frequently go over the top in their determination to ram home their opinions but the gentleman who wrote to the Sporting Life last summer complaining about Stuart Webster's riding of Blyton Lad positively made the blood boil.

The writer implied that Webster had used his stick both too liberally and too fiercely and that he should have received spontaneous punishment from the stewards on duty at the meeting.

Not only was the actual charge without foundation but the letter was a scurrilous attack on one of the finest horsemen in the business. Stuart Webster is rightly acknowledged as an outstanding educator of two year olds. Together with his girl friend Julie Craze he has been running a thriving livery stable for several years and his services are in frequent demand by trainers requiring a mature hand to guide their precocious youngsters.

With regard to his riding of Blyton Lad, one only has to glance at the form book to realise that this is one of the most successful and longstanding partnerships of modern day sprinting.

Stuart Webster has ridden the massively built 17 hands gelding since early in his three year old days. The pair of them have now won ten times from 37 outings, finishing in the frame on no less than 25 occasions and amassing over £145,000 in prize money.

No-one knows more intimately how to get the best from Blyton Lad and if the writer of the original letter had bothered to delve into the formbook, he would have discovered that Blyton Lad needs to be stoked along early in his races to get into contention. Not only is he one of the tallest horses in training, he is also among the most powerfully built sprinters around and to generate enough impetus to keep him in touch requires an all action effort from the rider almost as soon as the stalls open.

Blyton Lad cost a modest 5,200 guineas as a yearling the Addleshaws have owned him all his racing career and Stuart Webster has partnered him to all his victories to date. Blyton Lad has enjoyed less stability from the training angle. He has been prepared by five different trainers and has been under the care of Geoff Oldroyd since moving from Maurice Camacho in the Spring.

The gigantic son of Skyliner made his race course debut in a two year old maiden event at Beverley in August 1988.

Partnered by Steve Horsfall he ran unplaced but on his only subsequent outing of his juvenile career Blyton Lad's promise did not escape the eagle eye of Raceform's Ivor Markham.

Starting at 50-1 for the Division 1 of the EBF Kegsworth Maiden over seven furlongs, Markham reflected, "he stuck to his task gamely (when headed two furlongs out) and will find easier opportunities".

There might be a question mark about the racereaders latter observation but Blyton Lad clearly revealed potential from the start.

Ironically that Leicester race was won by Michael Stoute's Magical Strike, who cost 2.1 million dollars and never raced in this country after his three year old career.

Bawtry trainer John Balding was responsible for Blyton Lad throughout his first three seasons.

It was down to John to persuade his fast growing gelding to overcome a phobia of the whole starting procedure.

Blyton Lad had been withdrawn at the start of one of his two year old engagements. He was to incur the anxiety of both his connections and the starting stall team in four of his first five outings as a three year old but despite this frustrating aversion Blyton Lad continued to show ability once the race had got underway. He made late headway to finish third over six furlongs at Thirsk and was by no means disgraced in handicap company over longer distances.

Stuart Webster took over in the saddle for the 5 furlong Doncaster Writers' Handicap in late June and Blyton Lad registered the first success of his career, closing on the leaders two out and running on stoutly to force his head in front in the shadow of the post.

Blyton Lad was returned at 25/1 and beat Denham Green by 1 1/2 lengths with Craft Express a neck away third.

Webster, now in his thirty eighth year, recalls those early days with mixed feelings.

"Firstly there was the doubt about his proper trip. Blyton Lad had the physique of a potential three mile chaser and there were plenty of "advisors" who felt that he was sure to need a mile or more even as an early three year old. John had been trying him over six furlongs to a mile, but he ran prominently until passing the two furlong marker before stopping as though he had met a brick wall. I came along at the right time. He came back to the minimum distance for Doncaster and bolted in."

Webster's next worry was Blyton Lad's dislike of the preliminaries. "He started getting steamed up in the paddock", remembers Stuart. "He hated being mounted and if he caught sight of me in my racing silks he'd immediately begin sweating up and playing merry hell. I got the habit of hiding in the crowd then once the bell to mount had been rung I would wait my moment and jump aboard without him seeing me".

Fellow jockeys reckoned that Stuart was too brave for his own good but he had always had a knack with difficult horses and further more Stuart was convinced that once cured of his initial fears, Blyton Lad would have the ability to go right to the top.

"I had this sixth sense about him", continues Webster. "And I was right too. If it hadn't been for Blyton Lad, I'd have packed in the riding at least a couple of seasons ago".

Mind you Blyton Lad made Webster work for the reward. Though cajoled into leaving the paddock by Stuart's sudden rodeo like high jumping, he would sweat profusely all the way to the start before trying everyone's temper with his unruly behaviour at the stalls.

"If I remember correctly he was twice withdrawn at the start as a four year old, "relates Webster," and on other occasions he would do his best to force his way out once the gate had been shut behind him. It was claustrophobia of a type. He was over 17 hands and the stalls gave him that "caged in" feeling. he's perfectly OK nowadays but it took eighteen months to get him by the ears and hold on to his bit to keep him under control until the stalls open. The handlers have done a great job with him too".

Blyton Lad won twice more as a three year old at Redcar and Newbury. He ended the season being narrowly beaten in the 6 furlong Remembrance Day Stakes at Doncaster establishing in doing so, a precedent that he has followed in each of his last two campaigns.

1990 did not get off "to a flying start" in any sense of the phrase. Blyton Lad spent a whole minute with both hind legs off the ground wedged in the stalls before the Field Marshal Stakes. He had attempted to force his way out the back door and once extricated from the tangle was "withdrawn lame!"

By now however Stuart's patient persistence was beginning to pay dividends and Blyton Lad was becoming a character whom punters were beginning to trust with thier hard earned cash.

A pattern of engagements was also emerging, a sequence that Blyton Lad has followed to the current season.

Spring sees the giant strides devouring the Rowley Mile (or at least part of it) in the Palace House Stakes, then it is down to Sandown for the Temple Stakes followed by a visit to Goodwood for the King George.

Blyton Lad has frequently gone close without winning in all these competitive sprints but the autumn has been the time to tackle the bookmakers.

Brave efforts in the Nunthorpe and the Scarbrough Stakes

give advance warning of impending success at Newmarket and Doncaster. Blyton Lad won the Rous Stakes at Newmarket three times on the trot, 1990, 1991 and 1992 and was only shaded out of the winners circle last October when he was arguably just short of his best, having been passed fit to run by his vet only 48 hours before the race.

The gelding invariably goes close to winning the Bentick Stakes at Newmarket as well and has ended his last two seasons with success in the Remembrance Day Stakes at Town Moor.

A difference of opinion between owner and trainer led to Blyton Lad leaving John Balding to join Will Pearce for the start of the 1991 season.

The latter's apparent difficulty in sorting out his financial liabilities leading up to his tragic death in the summer of 1992 has tended to obscure the fact that he was a genuinely talented trainer.

Under his guidance and encouragement Blyton Lad finally overcame his dread of the starting stalls and ran a tremendous race in the Keeneland Nunthorpe stakes at York to finish third behind Sheikh Albadou and Paris House.

Third in a finish of heads to Notley in the Scarbrough Stakes, he was to reverse the placings with Richard Hannon's sprinter and gain deserved reward in the Roos Stakes the following month.

Next June, Will Pearce had Blyton Lad 'spot on' for The Kings Stand at Royal Ascot only to bring about his own end with a shot gun days before the race.

Ben Beasley gallantly filled the breach but there was to be no fairytale ending for the hard working head lad.

Blyton Lad was badly hampered well before half way and never got back into the race.

The owners, keen to find a settled home for their star, opted to remove him from Hambleton House and send him to Maurice Camacho. The decision paid off handsomely.

Blyton Lad won five times for The Malton trainer and on the rare occasions that he ran down the field, there were genuine excuses.

Blyton Lad broke a blood vessel and had to be pulled up in last year's Duke of York Stakes and was later forced to bypass the Hazelwood Foods Sprint Cup because "the scope" revealed "a dirty throat".

"Bursting" at York's May meeting was a major worry. For a while it seemed that Blyton Lad was finished as a major sprint performer but the Addleshaws and their trainer turned every stone to effect a recovery and their pride and joy made a spectacular recovery to finish the season firing on all cylinders.

Blyton Lad spent his Christmas holidays with Stuart Webster at his livery stable.

"He's been coming her since we started", says Webster. "He enjoys the break and this time we were able to send him back to Maurices's raring to go".

Blyton Lad had never won before June until this spring but first time out this April he trotted up in a Conditions Race at Thirsk causing Camacho to exclaim "He's a lovely horse to look after, a class horse who trains himself. It's the other 20 that I have to worry about".

In fact shortly after making that remark Maurice found himself without Blyton Lad. The giant sprinter left his yard as suddenly as he had arrived. Blyton Lad had just finished 6th to Lochsong in the Palace House Stakes - disappointing but not disastrous. Camacho felt that his feet had been troubling him since he'd won at Thirsk where the ground had been on the fast side of good.

One of the difficulties with Blyton Lad is his liking for firm ground. He is such a massive individual that he is prone to jarring his feet when travelling at racing pace.

Blyton Lad is now under the care of Geoff Oldroyd, the former north country jockey who is enjoying his second stint as a trainer.

Geoff sent out Blyton Lad to finish runner up to Lochsong in the Kings Stand Stakes but since then the 8 year old has failed to reach the first three in a series of Group class sprints. In his latest outing Blyton Lad and the indefatigable Webster came home in sixth place behind Misteropogigo in the Doncaster Bloodstock Sales Scarborough stakes. They were beaten less than four lengths.

Blyton Lad was due to reappear in his favourite Rous stakes at Newmarket's Cambridgeshire meeting but pre-race scoping discovered mucus in his tubes and he was an absentee. Sadly Blyton Lad died on the gallops as this book went to press. He will be sorely missed.

LUCKY PARKES

The temptation to look back in racing is hard to resist. Jockeys shouldn't make it a habit and trainers who live in the past soon lose their owners.

Perhaps the least likely to fall into this trap is Jack Berry, though even he will find it difficult to forget Paris House, the front running grey who has now retired to stand at the Corbally Stud at a fee of IR £3,500.

Paris House would have made an ideal subject for this book. he was bought for 5000 guineas and when his racing career came to an end after finishing runner up to Lochsong in the 1993 Keeneland Nunthorpe Stakes he had won 9 races and netted a total of £263,246 in win and place prize money.

Jack Berry will not forget Paris House; indeed he has already sent Petite D'Argent across to Co Kildare to be covered by his former star. In the meantime he will be working ceaselessly to find a successor and the probable candidate is Lucky Parkes, already the winner of thirteen races and only twice out of the first three in seventeen outings as a two and three year old.

When one considers that the first of those occasions was a creditable fifth to Lyric Fantasy in the 1992 Queen Mary Stakes at Royal Ascot and the second an equally sound fifth behind Tropical, in the Group 3 Arthur Guinness EBF Flying Five Stakes at Leopardstown, the chances are that Lucky

Parkes will more than fit the bill.

Like Paris House, the filly possesses searing speed. Normally she hits the starting gate and runs but ironically two of her defeats last summer came about because she was slow into her stride.

Lucky Parkes appeared to hesitate at the start of the Advanced Micro Devices Stakes, a listed race at Sandown in July and was beaten into third place behind Lochsong.

She was even slower out of the stalls at Leopardstown in September when fifth to Tropical.

Jack Berry explains, "There is nothing complicated about this filly. She is a dedicated professional who knows her job. She can be a bit edgy at the start but that's only because she's aware that she's about to be asked to go about her business. What the filly wants to do is to go straight in and come straight out."

If she has to hang about in the stalls then we begin to get anxious. In Ireland the starter hadn't received our message and Lucky Parkes was among the first to be loaded. She went 'bananas' and lost the race before she'd begun.

Pat Eddery was riding Lucky Parkes at Sandown and Lester Piggott had the mount in the Flying Five. To suggest that either of these two great jockeys were caught napping would be ridiculous but the incidents do underline the value of a top class stable jockey.

John Carroll, whose ability was advertised to a wider audience last season by the decision of John Gosden among others to put him up on fancied spare rides when available, never fails to work every lot on 'gallops' morning at

Cockerham. He is accustomed to each horse's individual quirks and in their turn they respond to his familiar touch. Make no mistake John Carroll's presence in the saddle freqently provides the cutting edge where it matters the most in the starting stalls.

Lucky Parkes is owner bred by Cheshire based farmer Joe Heler. She is the third foal of Summerhill Spruce whom Heler bought after she'd raced with promise as a juvenile and had won a 6f Seller at Ripon the following season.

Joe is into farming in a major way. He fattens upwards of 6000 bacon pigs every year, runs the largest independant cheese dairy in Britain and 300 dairy cattle are milked on his two farms at Audlem every morning.

Joe Heler is also a 'lucky' owner. Miss Parkes may not have been any great shakes but Lucky Parkes half sister Bella Parkes, by Tina's Pet won three races as a two year old last summer before meeting a slight setback and is now back in training at Cockerham.

"I've also got Sergeant Parkes with Jack", continues Joe. "He's doing well and seems to be highly regarded."

Lucky Parkes realised a life long ambition for her owner in 1992 when she landed the Lily Agnes Stakes at Chester's May Meeting.

"Chester is my local meeting". adds Joe Heler, "It was a tremendous thrill to see my colours carried to victory there and then I had the extra bonus of watching Bella Parkes do the same thing last summer".

Lucky Parkes is by Full Extent, the American bred stallion now standing in Shropshire whose victories for Steve Norton included the 1981 Gimcrack Stakes. Full Extent has yet to prove a noted success at stud but Jack Berry trains Satisfied Prince a Full Extent two year old who won at Ripon in April for Bernard Hathaway and this speedy colt looks well above average.

Lucky Parkes made an immediate impact as a juvenile, running up a quick hatrick on tight circuits like Catterick and Chester. She then proved her versatility by staying on in resolute fashion in the Queen Mary before winning the Ripon Horn Blower Stakes in August.

This was a thoroughly deserved success because the filly made every yard of the running to withstand the powerful late thrust of both Ansellman and Night Melody.

After she had landed the Lily Agnes at Chester by three quarters of a length from Richard Hannon's Risk Me's Girl, her trainer remarked, "She's a nervous type but she can trap as fast as my greyhound, Lisnakill Wish!"

The comparison was no insult. Lisnakill Wish was one of the top greyhound jumpers in the country until he collapsed and died of a heart attack.

He'd just pulled up after winning by eight lengths in record time. His replacement Jet On Sparkie has gone on to win nine races but Jack still regards Lisnakill Wish as the class performer.

Lucky Parkes has made striking physical progress since her early two year old days. She is no longer "a nervous type" but rather a strong, powerfully made filly with more than a touch of 'presence' about her appearance.

Last summer she progressed with each run. I had the privilege of watching her at close quarters in both her wins at Newcastle.

In late June at the Northumberland Plate fixture Lucky Parkes looked sharp and alert in the paddock but out on the course she allowed John Carroll to drop her out behind the pace setting Stack Rock before quickening smoothly below the distance to score with a degree of comfort.

This was no mean victory considering the runner up's subsequent success and when Lucky Parkes returned to Gosforth Park in October she stamped her quality on all around her.

John Carroll wasn't hanging about on this . Rightly considering that Lucky Parkes was the best horse in the contest, he encouraged her to find her stride from the start and the filly duly spreadeagled her field to win decisively with her head in her chest.

Lucky Parkes had developed into a strikingly attractive well made filly by the autumn of 1993.

In the spring Jack Berry reported that she had continued to mature. He described her as "bigger and more beautiful than ever". and was equally enthusiastic about the turn of foot that she had been showing on the all weather at Moss Side stables.

In a recent "Trainer File" interview published in the Racing Post, Jack had this to say; "Now this is a good filly. She's very, very fast. I think there is a right good race in her here or abroad if she gets the rub of the green".

Lucky Parkes opening race was due to be the East Ridings Stakes, a conditions event at Beverley on Grand National Saturday but the meeting was cancelled because the ground was waterlogged.

"I have to admit using the odd piece of bad language when I heard the news", recalls Jack Berry. "The filly was never better and the race conditions, to say nothing of the prize, were all in our favour.

We had to go back to the drawing board but I saw a suitable alternative at Bath and she did the job well. The need to win 'Black Type' is imperative. Lucky Parkes should prove a most valuable proposition 'for the paddocks' but before then there are plenty more decent races for her to win".

1994 has not been the 'luckiest' of seasons for 'Parkes'.

After her Bath victory she had a difference of opinion with the starting stalls at the same West Country track and was withdrawn.

The ground was too soft at Sandown for the Group 2 Tripleprint Temple Stakes and since then the Cockerham filly has been engaged in a series of head to head clashes with Ya Malak and Sheila's Secret

Lucky Parkes gained her second win of the season in a Class C conditions stakes at Sandown in June. Ya Malak was runner up.

'Pip' Payne's gelding then exacted revenge at Nottingham and Chester relegating Lucky Parkes to second place.

In August Sheila's Secret twice kept Joe Heler's heroine out of the winner's enclosure until a combination of good to firm ground and an eight pound pull enabled Lucky Parkes to make it third time lucky at Leicester in September when she made all the running in the hands of Gary Hind to win The

James Whitaker Conditions stakes by a cosy half length. Last time out Lucky Parkes finished 2nd at Gosforth Park behind Night Melody.

Lucky Parkes has now won thirteen races collecting £67,936 in prize money. That elusive listed race victory can only be a matter of time.

MAJED

The yellow and black checked jacket of Laurel Leisure Limited are among the best known colours in the North so familiar in fact that a certain commentator is regularly tempted to refer to their runners as "Laurel Leisure" whenever they appear.

This same caller alluded to Surrey "Racing" throughout the contest at Newcastle last autumn in which The Laurel "yellow and black strip" was actually worn by the runner up, Surrey "Dancer"!

Such an error will not be committed where Majed is concerned. This admirably tough five year old horse and I use the word advisedly as Majed remains an entire orginally cost IR 5,000 as a foal and was subsequently claimed by Andrew Hoyle, the mastermind behind the success of Laurel Leisure for £10,000 after running down the field at Newmarket in the Summer of 1992.

Already this sum looks cheap and should Majed go on to figure prominently in next years Champion Hurdle, the claiming price would take on the identity of 'the bargain of the nineties'.

Andrew Hoyle as always been an astute Judge of form. As racing editor of the Lancaster Evening Post; his tips had a wide following in the Red Rose country and his appetite for multiple ownership was whetted during his time in the editor's chair.

Andrew recalls "the paper had a filly called Miss L.E.P. , syndicated with Jack Berry and she was followed by several others who carried the colours of the readers.

"I managed the paper's horse, got to know Jack Berry pretty well and fianlly decided to go it alone and start my own racing club".

Laurel Leisure now boasts some 2000 members each paying a modest £75.20 plus VAT, to enjoy the privilege of co-ownership for a twelve month period from December 1st to the end of the following November.

In 1993 Laurel Leisure povided its members with 16 wins and Majed was a major contibutor to that score. With the retirement of the club's evergreen standard bearer, Laurel Queen he now becomes the members particular pride and joy.

Unlike other syndicate directors Hoyle fights shy of gambling on the yearling market. Laurel own the token two year old but their success comes in the main from older horses usually claimed with enviable skill by their organizer.

Majed ran three times as a two year old showing more than a modicum of promise. Trained by Neville Callaghan the colt was described by Timeform as "useful looking and a good walker". he was allotted a rating of 78p.

Both comment and rating have stood the test of time. With hindsight too, Majed's performance in finishing third in the Royston Stakes at Newmarket was an eye opener.

Ridden by Emma O'Gorman he tracked the leaders throughout and though only able to run on at one pace close home,

Majed got within five lenghs of the runner up Cruachan who would have been a leading contender for the 1991 Ever Ready Derby had he not chipped a bone on his off fore and had to miss the race.

Majed ran consistently as a three year old but it was not until late October that he finally lost his maiden tag in the Vauxhall Handicap at Yarmouth. Backed down to 2/1 favourite Majed earned Sheik Althami, his owner, the princely sum of £2,735.80.

During the winter of 1991-92 he was tried over hurdles but did not seem to stay the trip.

Andrew Hoyle first sat up and took notice on a cold wet afternoon the following April. He. recalls "It was a typical early seasson mud bath at Hamilton. The club had Laurel Queen running in the Standard Life Handicap. She started 5/2 favourite but we knew that she'd find it hard work winning because the ground was much too soft."

"I was also interested in the performance of Rose Glen because Laurel had leased her some time back and her trainer Alan Bailey fancied her chances".

In the event Rose Glen started a well backed 4/1 chance but despite running on gamely could never match strides with Majed who won by five lengths, with Jason Weaver looking round for non existent dangers from a long way out.

"Majed made a favourable impression on me then and there". continues Andrew "and I filed him away in my mind as a horse to watch".

Not long after Majed renewed rivalry with Laurel Queen in different circumstances at Beverley.

"It was a claimer", remembers Andrew Hoyle. "The ground was firmish and Laurel Queen came out best in a three way photo. Majed ran from an outside draw, didn't like the ground but was only beaten two short heads into third place. Come to think about it, I must have considered making a claim for him then but didn't!"

Hoyle bided his time.

"I noted that Majed was running in a claimer at Newmarket's late June meeting. I had to be at Newcastle but Keith Reveley was there and I asked him to put in a claim. I didn't expect Majed to win because the ground was too fast and I thought we might be lucky."

Andrew's judgement was spot on. Majed finished eighth, making some headway from three furlongs out but never getting close enough to lay down a challenge.

Ironically the winner, Bowden Boy, was also trained by Neville Callaghan but the Newmarket trainer didn't bother to put in a friendly claim for Majed and Laurel Leisure's new purchase joined Mary Reveley at Saltburn.

The chestnut made his debut for the Groundhill Farm team in The Juddmonte Claiming Stakes at Haydock in early August. John Lowe rode and Majed delighted connections with an eyecatching fifth to Rambo's Hall.

Hopes were high that the Laurel members would have a day to remember at Chester later in the month but the rain, promised so confidently by Michael Fish, did not arrive until the evening.

Majed finished third, beaten three quarters of a length and a neck by the battle hardened pair of Silver Samurai and Causley.

Disappointed but not down hearted was the general reaction. The failure of the promised rain to materialize in time for the race had left the ground a shade too fast and to add to the colt's difficulties he was drawn on the outside and had to come wide off the final bend.

Conditions were perfect for Majed at Haydock's late September fixture. Mary Reveley had three fancied runners that murky autumn afternoon. Majed lined up for the Leigh Handicap, an amateur riders event at the Lanchashire course, Sunderland Echo was well regarded at Redcar and Sharpalto, partnered for the first time by Michael Kinane carried the Saltburn hopes in the Festival Handicap at Ascot.

Long time members of the Laurel Leisure team still recall the day with exuberance.

The club had been on a stable visit to Groundhill Farm in the morning and the great majority of them combined all three Reveley horses in each way patents.

It was to prove a long nail biting afternoon. Sharpalto cruised home, landing the Festival Handicap hard held by three and half lengths at 11/1. That win took place at 1.30 pm.

Majed did not run until 3.15. Bearing in mind his two recent runs, Majed went off at a generous price of 15/2. the Reveley's stable amateur and assistant trainer Mark Buckley, an accomplished rider in his own right, obeyed his instuctions to the letter.

He held up his mount in mid division, made his move entering the final furlong and pushed Majed a length clear near the line. Two legs of the double already in the bag at odds of 11/1 and 15/2. The third and decisive part of the patent, Sunderland Echo was not due to come under orders until 5.15.

The story does not relate how the Luarel members spent the intervening two hours but those still at Haydock half an hour after the last race crowded round the television monitors amid the carpet of discarded betting slips and cigarette butts to watch Sunderland Echo bid to win Redcar's Apprentice Handicap.

The locally trained horse started an even money favourite but his supporters frame of mind was not eased by the knowledge that the entire course at Redcar was enshrouded by an inpenetrable sea fret. Not even the race course commentator could shed much light on the progress of the contest but when the leaders finally emerged form the clinging mist, there Oh Joy on Joy was Sunderland Echo leading the charge. Driven out, by 17 year old Darren Moffatt, The gallant 'Jolly' passed the post in front with a length to spare over the chasing pack.

The treble was on the table and at a mouth watering price of 203/1. Days like that don't arrive often and young Darren was to play an increasingly important role in the development of Majed.

The teenager was in the saddle when the colt followed up successfully on the Knavesmire in October and the partnership has remained intact ever since.

The results do not require listing in detail but suffice it to say, Majed has raced seven times for Master Moffatt, has finished first past the post on four occasions and has never been far out of the money.

Mind you the margin of success has often been wafer thin and as Andrew Hoyle explains. "Darren has a magic touch with Majed but he's left our hearts in our mouths more than once". None more so than at Chester and Newcastle last autumn. A short head in each case and a very short head to boot.

Don't blame the man on top. Majed has a useful turn of foot but that burst of acceleration must not be used until the post is within spitting distance or he is in danger of tying up in front.

Majed has already been a remarkable success story for Laurel Leisure. Since being claimed at Newmarket he has won £20,532 on the flat and a further £22,837 under rules.

Arguably he was bought with hurdling at the top of the agenda and it cannot be stressed too highly how brilliantly he has been campaigned in this sphere.

Majed has run nine races over timber and has yet to finish out of the first two. In 1992-93 Mary Reveley trained him to win his first three novice hurdles off the reel. He was then narrowly held by the useful Arcot at Newcastle and had to run on unfavourable fast ground when going down by half a length to Bellton next time out at Nottingham Majed reversed that defeat in the Hennessy Cognac Special Novice Hurdle at Kelso and ended the campaign with a narrow defeat by Dancing Paddy in The Trillium Hurdle at Ascot.

"After what had been a busy summer on the flat, followed by seven races over hurdles, Majed was in need of a break", explains Andrew Hoyle. "He was turned out for the summer with a lovely lady in Cleveland. She is devoted to him and looks after him like a king." Majed returned to action last autumn and in brilliant order after a successful programme on the flat, went to Wetherby on Dec 4th for the A.T.S. Handicap Hurdle. Mark Buckley was on board and Majed was set to give Arcot, his most dangerous rival, six pounds.

From the commentator's eyrie high in the Wetherby grandstand the famous yellow and black checks could be easily picked out even in the gloom of a darkening December dusk.

Buckley could not prevent him surging to the front between the final two flights but he put down a stride before the last, went through the top and lost impetus.

The mistake handed the initiative back to Arcot, who must have started up the short Wetherby run in with an advantage of at least a length. It was not enough. Given a brief moment to collect himself, Majed rallied and quickened almost simultaneously, regained the lead in a couple of strides and won going away.

This was the sort of performance for which connections had hardly dared to hope. Major handicaps, even a shot at the Champion Hurdle seemed the natural progression but it was not to be.

The dreaded cough was circulating at Saltburn. Majed succumbed shortly after returning from Wetherby and did not pick up condition for two months.

The Tote Gold Hurdle at Newbury had been touted as his next objective but the trip had to be aborted.

Majed was not firing on all cylinders. The Champion Hurdle became the new target and Majed, now fully recovered, made the long journey south for a preliminary trial at Newbury only ten days before the festival. He finished second, beaten once again by Dancing Paddy.

The reason for this reverse was not long in coming. Majed had developed 'a leg'.

He spent all summer out at grass, being spoilt by all and sundry. The plan had been to bring him back in the autumn for a couple of races on the flat and then aim at the 1995 Champion hurdle. This could be premature. Majed is on the mend but Mary Reveley is inclined to extend his recovery span until next spring. "Hurdling puts a tremendous strain on the legs", she explains, "and I'd rather wait for the flat to start him off again".

There are no plans to geld Majed. The long term policy is to campaign the chestnut in Group races on the flat. "That would be after he's won at Cheltenham", say Andrew Hoyle with a gleam in his eye.

"I would like to go for a race like the John Porter at Newbury next spring and advance from there. I think Majed has all the qualities required for a top class dual purpose stallion. Everyone says he's a super horse to handle with a lovely gentle temperament. It would be an awful shame to geld him and lose his stud value".

Majed thankfully is unaware that such drastic thoughts are even being considered. He is chomping grass and thinking of soft ground in the spring.

Mrs Reveley meanwhile is quietly optimistic that 'the leg' will make a complete recovery and that Majed will be back before the end of the year to fulfil his potential as a Champion Hurdle contender, even if the date of the triumph will now be March 1996.

One thing is for sure, Majed seems destined to continue Laurel Leisure's remarkable run of success with the horses in their ownership

MISTER BAILEYS

Mister Baileys was bought as a foal for 10,000 guineas. Owner Paul Venner made the purchase and then submitted the chestnut to the October Yearling sales at Newmarket.

No one was interested in the slightly gawky boy with a lot of white about him but Venner took the opposite view and brought him back again for an additional 500 guineas.

After Mister Baileys had run third to Erhaab in the Homeowners Dante Stakes at York, his prize money tally stood at £232,703 and there was a lot more to come.

Whispers about the colt's ability had been circulating for several weeks before he made his debut at Newcastle in June 1993.

He was reputed to be "Johnston's best two year old; something special".

It was ironic then to find Mister Baileys taking a significant walk in the betting before his first race.

There is something refreshing to find a classic winner beginning his career in an event called the Federation Brewery L.C.L. Pils Lager Stakes! Mister Baileys looked magnificent in the paddock - a rangy powerful sort with tremendous scope. Perhaps the fact that he was so powerfully framed persuaded connections that he would need the outing but punters did not want to know - this one excluded!

The Middleham Colt was introduced at 5/2 and eased out to as long as 6/1 before attracting sufficient late support to shorten to fives just before the off.

The race was a non event. Mister Baileys broke smartly, aimed for the centre of the track and dwarfed his rivals from pillar to post.

Dean McKeown did not ask him to quicken until approaching the two furlong maker but the response was immediate with Mister Baileys lengthening his stride to storm home seven lengths clear of the favourite Level Sands.

Those responsible for passing the word that the Middleham colt was just here for the exercise glanced furtively towards the exit. Those who had trusted the evidence of their own eyes trotted gleefully towards the ring.

Reports of Mister Baileys potential had clearly reached Newbury when he reappeared for the Donnington Castle stakes. He again impressed paddock watchers and started a well backed 11/10 favourite having been put in at 7/4.

The Donnington will not go into the McKeown scrapbook as one of his more accomplished races but to be fair his fellow jockeys made a meal of Dean's hesitation at the start.

Instead of punching Mister Baileys out of the stalls and quickly asserting a favourable pitch on or near the stands rails, Dean settled Mister Baileys behind the leading pair and then allowed himself to become the meat in the proverbial sandwich as his rivals closed in.

Mister Baileys had nowhere to go and had McKeown not

taken the law into his own hands, gone for a narrow gap on his outside and forced Mister Baileys to drive through it, the colt would have had to sit in behind and finish out of the first three with his rider motionless in the saddle.

Classic Sky and Walter Swinburn took the prize by a cheeky half length with Mister Baileys fairly eating up the ground close home a short head third behind Cult Hero.

Dean McKeown was interviewed by The Stewards and the partnership made a quick return visit southwards to secure The Lanson Vintage Champagne Stakes at Glorious Goodwood.

Punters steamed in to retrieve their Newbury losses and picked up with interest. Dean made his move wide of the rails passing the two furlong marker and Mister Baileys eased home 2½ lengths ahead of Prince Baba with the unbeaten Lomas well behind in third.

The Goodwood race was over seven furlongs and despite the trainer's expressed opinion that Mister Baileys needed every yard of that trip he was declared for the six furlong Gimcrack Stakes at York's August meeting.

Paul Venner's influence appears to have been the decisive factor here and predictably Mister Bailey's could not sustain the pace.

Rather surprisingly promoted the 15/8 market leader, Mister Baileys led until two furlongs out but did not have the extra acceleration to repulse the challenges queuing up behind. Dean McKeown compounded the error by losing his whip at the furlong marker and Mister Baileys could only finish sixth at least seventh lengths adrift of the winner Turtle Island.

By September Dean McKeown had left to ride in Hong Kong and Frankie Dettori took his place on Mister Baileys for the Royal Lodge at Ascot.

The colt's appearance in the paddock was as imposing as ever with the exception that traces of the ring worm infection he had picked up around the time of his substandard run at York were still evident.

Mark Johnston never used the ringworm as an excuse but Mister Baileys' work was temporarily interrupted and he might just have needed the outing at Ascot.

Dettori cruised up to the leaders on the outside of the home turn and took up the running below the distance. For a couple of strides it seemed that Mister Baileys would stretch clear of his rivals but in the end Dettori had to keep his mount up to his work.

At the post Mister Baileys had half a length to spare over Concordial with Overbury another short head away third. The distance was a mile and the Middleham colt saw the trip out well.

Johnston was of the opinion that Mister Baileys needed ten furlongs and would certainly stay a mile and a half. The Derby was mooted as the probable target.

The winter was cold and wet at Kingsley House. The early spring a shade warmer but still very wet.

The Johnston horses were clocking up the winners on the all weather and Jason Weaver had made a great start as stable jockey.

Mister Baileys had strengthened up during the close season

but he has never enjoyed working on the all-weather strip and connections were worried that he would not be forward enough to do himself justice in the Madagans 2000 Guineas.

"I was getting anxious", admits Mark. "I'd already decided that he'd need to go straight to Newmarket without a preliminary race but the rain didn't help."

Then at the crucial moment the sun shone. Mister Baileys showed his appreciation with a sparkling piece of fast work on the grass gallops with Beware of Agents who began the exercise with an advantage of a clear ten lengths but was remorselessy cut down and finally overtaken.

Post-race gallops were then arranged at both Thirsk and Ripon. Those who watched the workouts were deeply impressed and hastened to get in touch with their credit accounts.

Confidence rose and events proved how justified the optimisim had been. Mister Baileys started at 16/1. Always lying handy, he hit the front with three furlongs to travel, was joined by Grand Lodge passing the furlong marker but stayed on resolutely to withstand the challenge by a neck.

The 2000 Guineas had returned to the North for the first time since George Boyd's Rockavon had travelled South from Dunbar to triumph in the hands of Norman Stirk. Rockavon won at 66/1.

Mister Baileys was returned at sixteens and there was much celebration North of the Trent.

Mark Johnston announced that The Homeowners Dante Stakes would be the colt's next race and bookmakers promoted him top of the list for the Ever Ready Derby.

The Press were generous with their praise, saluting a new force on the centre stage of British flat racing. Those of us living in the North had realised that Mark Johnston was more than "a bit special" at least two seasons ago but it needs one major success to break down the barriers.

A classic winner is worth at least fifty ordinary scalps and Mister Baileys' Newmarket triumph could not have come at a more opportune moment either for Mark Johnston, Jason Weaver or for that matter the village of Middleham.

Johnston has always maintained that classic winners can be trained on the High Moor at Middleham just as easily as they can on the more fashionable gallops at Newmarket. He does not intend to be remembered as the man who trained Mister Baileys to win the 2000 Guineas. He wants and regards the colt's success as a precedent to other similar wins.

Owner Paul Venner has had horses in training with Mark right from the start. He is also Managing Director of Baileys Horse Foods-the company that supplies Johnson with the raw materials for all his horses' diets.

The expression is used advisedly for Mark, a qualified vet, co-operates in detail with Baileys' nutritional experts and has developed his own dietary system which is based on the practice of providing his horses with food that contains a high level of fat additives. The exact quantities and the frequency of each horse's meal is carefully balanced and given correctly. The Johnson diet ensures that his string not only look supremely well but also that they retain their form throughout the season.

This ability to bring his horses back to peak fitness so soon after a hard race is the quality that Jason Weaver most admires in his new guvnor.

It was palpably evident in the superb physical condition of Mister Baileys when he appeared in the paddock before the Dante. The colt had won the best turned out award at Newmarket and he looked magnificent at York.

The crucial question was one of stamina. Would Mister Baileys stay the extended 10 furlongs?

If he was going to last out the the full Derby distance then he must be seen to stay the shorter trip of the Dante.

In Middleham opinions differed about the colts optimum trip. Lennie Peacock, breeder of Tirol and very much an authority on blood lines maintained from the beginning that Mister Baileys would prove a specialist miler.

Mark Johnston was confident that his colt would stay 10 furlongs and was hopeful that he'd get the mile and a half.

His sire Robellino emulated Mister Baileys by winning The Royal Lodge but finished well in arrears in Shergar's Derby.

The dam Thimblerigger won over ten furlongs and Mister Baileys' three parts brother Cleavers Gate won over an extended 1m 6 furlongs at Catterick. The influence of Roberto in the pedigree also indicates that Mister Baileys should stay a mile and a half but sadly the Dante suggested otherwise.

Mister Baileys was lobbing on a tight rein approaching the two furlong marker but within another furlong he was flat to the boards and producing ˉothing. He finished third, beaten comfortably by both Erhaab and Weigh Anchor. The distances were 3½ lengths and 1 length. On the evidence of the

Dante, Mister Baileys failed to stay but as his trainer rightly points out he still finished a relatively close third to two of the finest colts in training and therefore had every right to take his chance at Epsom.

Mister Baileys ran very free at York. He had shown the same enthusiasm at Newmarket. If he was to play a major role in the Derby, then he would need to settle better in the early stages.

Mark Johnston did not enter Mister Baileys for the 1m St James Palace Stakes at Royal Ascot. There were several suitable races in France but only one Derby. Mister Baileys did not race again before the Derby.

Gary Ritchie, his lad, was confident that Mister Baileys would go on to win top class contests even if he failed to land the 'big one' at Epsom.

Ritchie has been "a lucky lad". Apart from Mister Baileys he has looked after both Quick Ransom and Marina Park. His ambition was to make the grade as a flat race jockey. He never quite made it in that direction but he is an invaluable work-rider and was responsible for warming up Mister Baileys in his final piece of work before the Guineas.

Gary was to prove supremely proud of Mister Baileys at Epsom even though his charge could only finish fourth.

Pre-race tactics were thrown out of the window as Mister Baileys took charge. He burst from the stalls and was already in clear pole position long before the field approached the descent to Tattenham Corner.

Jason Weaver sensibly gave him his head and for one glorious moment the impossible seemed attainable.

Mister Baileys was still in command, entering the final two furlongs but seconds later his legs turned to jelly and he could do no more.

Mister Baileys finished fourth and Mark Johnston admitted later that he had never seen a more exhausted horse come off the course.

The colt was given a seven week rest before his next race, the Sussex Stakes at Goodwood. Physically he looked magnificent but he was very much on his toes in the paddock and it was no surprise to see him set a blistering gallop as soon as the stalls opened.

Mister Bailey's speed helped set up a record time but once the others went past him between the last two furlongs he had nothing left in the tank.

Jason Weaver remarked "It was a great race. He picked up well but the others went past him as if he was standing still".

Mark Johnston discovered later that Mister Baileys had been struck into during the race. He said, "The colt took a bit of a knock on his off-fore leg and while that's not much of an excuse it might help to explain why he didn't quicken.

Having said that he set such a fantastic pace for the first three quarters of a mile that he just had nothing left in the end".

Defeat for a classic winner always comes as an anti-climax but it must not be forgotten that Mister Bailey's explosive speed both at Epsom and at Goodwood was the prime cause of those races producing such a thrilling outcome.

Mister Baileys has been sold to stand at the National Stud next year with Paul Venner retaining a share of the action. He was due to reappear in the Queen Elizabeth II Stakes at Ascot's Festival of Racing but had to be treated for colic ten days before the race.

Mister Baileys was being re-routed to the Dubai Champion Stakes at Newmarket with the possibility of the Breeders Cup Mile as a final throw. Sadly the leg that had been hurt during the Sussex Stakes began to swell up again during September and despite medication continued to cause problems.

Mister Bailey's future now lies at stud. In a deal said to be worth around three quarters of a million pounds the colt has been sold to the National Stud. He will stand at an expected fee of £6,500 (Oct 1st) and it is intended that he will cover some 60 mares in his first season. Paul Venner has retained a half share in his classic winner.

STACK ROCK

The phrase 'a family stable' can sometimes describe a multi-tude of amateur transgressions. It can bring to mind a macho father, his tired wife and brood of assorted off spring all going their separate ways, believing that each can cope better and more efficiently than the other members of the family -
The riding gets done but the more mundane activities such as 'mucking out' tend to be left to the youngest who will then rebel by withdrawing their labour.

I exaggerate of course and there are many family units that are paragons of efficiency in which the horses thrive because they are part and parcel of the system and are treated as members of the household.

The stable run by Eric and Sue Alston with vital assistance from their son Mark is an ideal example of the successful family network.

Edges Farm Stables in the village of Longton, not far from Preston houses some thirty horses, all of which receive the same loving care that the children of the happiest family would expect as their natural right.

Eric Alston learnt his trade with Walter Wharton, for whom he worked four years. He was a useful rider but never going to make the big time as a professional jockey.

He made the sensible decision to return to farming rather than live out an impossible dream and having organised his life in an orderly and profitable manner picked up again where he had left off.

Eric first took out a trainer's licence in 1981. His initial horses were mostly a mixed bunch of jumpers and it wasn't until the end of the eighties that he began to turn his attention to the flat.

"Nowadays I hardly train any jumpers at all," says Eric. "I've realised that preparing horses to run on the flat is both easier and more profitable. You don't get the injuries and with Wolverhampton's all weather track opening up this last winter, I've begun to put all my eggs into the same basket".

The change of emphasis has been accelerated by a serious traffic accident which ended Mark Alston's career as a jump jockey.

Mark now adopts the roles of Head Lad and principal work rider and assistant trainer. His judgement about a horse's fitness is spot on.

The progress of the Alston's close knit family stable can be monitored by results. In 1989, the family sent out one winner on the flat. This became six in 1990, double the amount in 1991, fifteen in 1991 and twenty last year. The tally for the current campaign is already 17 and Stack Rock, the stable star has played no part in the total.

Now seven years old, Stack Rock has always been physically robust: By Ballad Rock out of a Nebbiolo mare called One Better, she cost peanuts as a yearling; 1,200 Irish Punts to be exact and was sent to the Alstons as a backward three year old.

Eric recalls "we were sent her by a regular contact who thought that she had the potential to make a successful hurdler. He had liked the look of her and had bought her cheaply out of a field near Thurles. Actually the owner was a 'dogs man'. Frank McKevitt, Stack Rock's original purchaser, himself a great greyhound enthusiast, advised him to take the horse and recommended he go to Eric Alston to be trained".

The Alstons took possession of Stack Rock as an unraced three year old in October 1990. By the start of the 1994 flat race season, the mare had won nine times from 42 outings, been placed on nineteen other occasions and netted £120,505 in win and place prize money.

Sue Aston takes up the story, "She has been the most marvellous horse to have in the stable. She loves her work, eats her head off and is absolutely no sort of trouble to train".

Early on the family accepted the official verdict that Stack Rock would eventually go jumping but their opinion took a nasty jolt when the filly began to outpace their recognised sprinters on the home gallops.

Timeform's Racehorses of 1990 had other ideas. I quote "first form in maidens when winning 16 - runner event at Southwell in November by one and a half lengths from Gaiety: ran moderately in handicap there two weeks later. Suited by a mile".

Even Homer can nod and the form students from Halifax had revised their opinion by the end of the following year. They referred to the 4 year old as "ideally suited by 6 furlongs; goes well with forcing tactics, tough, genuine and consistent" - words that would be certain to put a smile on any owner's face and brought a wide grin to the expressions of the

70

members of the Castle Racing Syndicate, who were now the proud owners of the mare.

The syndicate will no doubt have been watching the recently screened "Lifeboat Soap" on BBC1 not just because the series was filmed in Wales but also because they themselves are all connected with the Lifeboat service.

The four owners all hail from Little Haven in Dyfed. They comprise the Landlord of the Castle Hotel, the local postmaster, a Texaco emloyee and the proprietor of a tool hire firm from Haverfordwest.

When they first joined together to buy Stack Rock, all four of them were members of the Little Haven Lifeboat crew, hence their colours of black with the orange disc.

So well has the mare performed for them that they invested in a second purchase, the four year old maiden Rosie O'Reilly. Sadly the filly proved slow and went to the sales in July.

The quartet from Dyfed named their original buy "Stack Rock" after the barren rock not far off the coast of Little Haven.

The rock may be unproductive but the horse has been far from unprofitable.

In only her second season (1991) she won three times over six furlongs and was in the first three on five other occasions.

Castle Racing travelled the length and breadth of Britain to watch her run; usually by train leaving the one and only bookmaker in Little Haven ruling the day that the syndicate had ever gone into ownership - so popular is Stack Rock that the whole community back her everytime she runs.

The mare first hinted at her quality when she led throughout to beat Mango Manila and Lallapaloosa in the £10,000 Palan Handicap at Ascot in July 1991.

Stack Rock appeared another five times that season and never ran a poor race. Eric Alston was still experimenting with her distance and immediately after Ascot, he brought her back to the minimum trip for the Coral Bookmakers sprint at Haydock, his local course.

Young Brett Doyle took the ride and Stack Rock made late headway to finish sixth, only beaten about three lengths. Those experienced sprint handicappers Cantoris, Croft Imperial and Viceroy occupied the first three positions.

Kieran Fallon, Stack Rock's regular pilot, was back in the saddle for the 6 furlong Lawrence Batley Handicap at York. Stack Rock had every chance but could not quicken. She finished a creditable fifth beaten less than 2 lengths. Alston then tried her over seven furlongs in the Kyoto Handicap at the St Leger meeting. The mare finished 4th to Perfolia having been outpaced over the last furlong.

A week later Stack Rock raced over six furlongs in the Five Ten Friday Handicap at Ayr - always prominent she led in the centre and held on gamely to account for Darakah and Forever Diamonds.

Fallon rode her with more patience at Newmarket in October, taking it up inside the final furlong and being all out to resist the powerful late challenge of Triviality and Snowgirl.

The handicapper got to the mare in 1992 but she still managed to win over an extended five furlongs at Newbury in the spring and was beaten only a length by Master Planner in the 6 furlong Eagle Lane Handicap at York's August meeting. The then little known five pound claimer Jason Weaver had the mount and Stack Rock could not quicken with the winner inside the final furlong.

Connections decided to go for black type in 1993 and Stack Rock answered their call in gallant sytle. She raced twelve times, winning four good class events and finishing runner up on five other occasions.

All courses come alike to this most genuine of mares who takes little training once she has blown away the winter cobwebs. The tight bends round the Roodeye suit her nicely and with the course a mere two hours journey from Little Haven, Chester is a popular venue for Castle Racing.

Stack Rock paid three visits in 1993 and duly completed the hat-trick. At the spring meeting she always had too much speed for Plain Fact and in July she had no difficulty giving away six pounds to Palacegate Episode in a Conditions Race.

In between times, partnered by Stephen Davies, the Newmarket based claimer, Stack Rock led inside the final furlong and held off the powerful challenge of Gorinsky to win by a short head.

Fast ground at Royal Ascot and the combination of a firm surface and a bad draw at Newcastle led to a couple of disappointments but Eric Alston waved the magic wand once more and the mare returned to her very best at Newmarket in late August.

The Hopeful Stakes, a listed race presented a serious challenge but as Simon Holt so graphically reported in the Sporting Life, "If medals for gallantry were handed out to racehorses, Stack Rock would have a chestful of them".

Starting at 9/1, she made all the running to provide the Alstons with their first listed race success and in the course of the final furlong courageously beat off the sustained challenges of Garah and King's Signet.

Eric had left his binoculars behind and when one of his horses burst a blood vessel in the opener the old cliche' of "bad news coming in threes" threatened to ruin his day.

Happily it was not to be and with Kieran Fallon riding a superlative finish Stack Rock kept all-comers at bay.

Kieran's fiery temperament causes him to be a more regular visitor to the stewards room than is ideal but there are few better jockeys to have on your side in a tight finish and Eric uses him whenever he is available.

Kieran knows Stack Rock like the back of his hand and the mare has always done her very best for the Irishman. The mare is also a trencherwoman of no small repute and at Newmarket had been 5kg heavier than her regular racing weight

"I was worrying that she had overdone it a shade", said Alston, "but the protein seemed to do the trick."

The Longton trainer now cast his net overseas and Stack Rock tackled the Group 3 Arthur Guinness EBF Flying Five Stakes at Leopardstown. Tropical was a warm favourite on the day and although the gallant visitor led until the distance she had no answer to the late surge of acceleration from Dermot Weld's high class filly and had to be content with second place.

The runner's up berth was also her fate in the twelfth and final race of an honourable season. There were some who felt that connections were flying too high when they declared Stack Rock for the Ciga Prix De L'Abbaye at Longchamp but the smile was on the other side of their faces as "the lass from Lancashire" ploughed bravely through the mud to take a thoroughly deserved second place behind Lochsong.

Stack Rock retained the runner's up berth by a shorthead from Monde Bleu with Group class sprinters of the calibre of Tropical, Zieten and Wolfhound well in arrears. The members of Castle Racing held their heads high and tucked into the caviar and champagne.

The mare enjoyed a long winters rest. She reappeared to finish down the field in both the Palace House Stakes at Newmarket and the Temple Stakes at Sandown before disappearing from the scene until late August.

The reason behind her comparative idleness was a trapped sciatic nerve. Eric Alston explains -

"Cash Asmussen, who rode her in the Temple, reported that she had never given him a proper feel' and thought that her back had been giving trouble. I had Mark Windsor, our back man, give the mare a careful examination and he discovered the root of the problem".

Stack Rock had regular treatment but the slight lameness persisted until the mid-summer.

The setback was frustrating but Alston was not over-anxious. Ground conditions would have been against Stack Rock for much of the summer and in any case the trainer had laid her out to win the Haydock Park Sprint Cup on the first Saturday in September.

Eric decided to give Stack Rock a preparatory race in the Hopeful Stakes at Newmarket and despite dropping out quickly from the two furlong marker, Jockey Philip Robinson thought she had done well.

Kieran Fallon was back on board for the Haydock Park Group One but Stack Rock never threatened. The following day she was retired and will spend the remainder of her life grazing peacefully at stud in Ireland.

FLAKEY DOVE

Watching Flakey Dove slouch round the Cheltenham paddock shortly before the Smurfit Champion Hurdle, I marked a cross against her name in the racecard and turned my attention towards finding the winner.

Ten minutes later the name of Flakey Dove was mentioned by the presenter of Festival Radio and I found myself saying that the mare had looked "hard trained and lethargic" in the paddock and that my overall impression was that she was feeling the effect of three energetic races.

I dismissed her chances. Not long after Flakey Dove scuttled bravely up the Cheltenham hill to record a famous victory and leave a certain paddock observer with a great deal of egg on his face.

The following morning a chance meeting with Mark Dwyer outside the weighing room made me feel a degree happier. Asked how he had felt when he first set eyes on Flakey Dove in the paddock before the contest, he replied "I wondered what I had let myself in for. She seemed disinterested, small and almost scrawny compared with the likes of Oh So Risky and Large Action,"

According to Richard Price, her trainer, that's the way she always looks when ready to run her heart out. That's exactly what she did at Cheltenham even to the extent of forcing her jockey to take a pull on the run to the second last.

Mark Dwyer recalls the moment. "She'd been travelling well all the way and was keen to go on down the hill but Mr Price had warned me not to get her head in front too early and I waited until after the last,"

The decision was entirely right. Once on the uphill run to the line. Mark asked Flakey Dove for her effort and the "Plain Jane" mare produced that crucial turn of foot that left her pursuers struggling in her wake.

Like her trainer, I had let her run unbacked. "Me and betting don't get on," admitted Richard Price in the winner's circle "but most of my friends backed her at 66/1".

The trouble is there are too many "Doves" nowadays and too many Prices as well. The dual families also live in Herefordshire and being a dyed in the wool northerner my wagers are restricted to anything trained the right side of the Trent.

Such an attitude wasn't always the case and back in the early sixties two horses never failed to fire the imagination. They were the almost white Magic Orb, trained by Alex Kilpatrick and Red Dove, the responsibility of Gordon Price. There was a touch of romance about her background and the fact that she ran 93 times in her career winning sixteen races and being placed on innumerable other occasions ensured a reasonable return.

Interest in the Price family continued to her daughter Grey Dove, mainly if memory serves me right because the grey was also ridden by Cecil Price, a carrot headed amateur who always had a struggle reaching the course in time to take the ride as he couldn't leave until all the cows had been milked.

Cecil's whereabouts remained a mystery until he suddenly reappeared at Warwick's late March meeting to welcome home his home bred 20/1 winner Spot The Dove.

Cecil apparently is a cousin of Richard but then there have been two Tom's and a Gordon just for starters.

Spot The Dove is also a cousin to Flakey Dove but what about Another Dove, Shadey Dove, Saucy Dove, Dextra Dove, Nimble Dove to say nothing of the tragic Jubilee Dove who "died in battle" from a broken neck.

Too many "Doves" to seriously keep tabs on. A silly reason not to back them and an unprofitable one too as according to present calculations the family have clocked up some 90 successes and they're still going strong for five hundred.

Like many of National Hunt's best loved breeding lines, the Dove dynasty begins with the proverbial "steal".

Flakey Dove's great gran-dam Cottage Lass was brought by Richard Price's grandfather Tom for £25 at Ludlow market. She was foaled in 1940, won point to points in Wales just after the war and would have been sent to the knacker had farmer Tom not stepped in with his bid.

Cottage Lass had broken down badly but Tom wanted a mare to breed from and she was by the famous Irish jumping stallion, Cottage. Nothing was known about the distaff side hence the ineligibility of the Dove family to make the official stud book.

Cottage Lass was sent to All Red, a local stallion. The result was Red Dove and the latter's daughter Shady Dove is the dam of Flakey Dove, who is owned by Richard Price's father Tom, the son of the original Tom - all very simple as one can see.

Richard's dad, now 70 years old and officially retired from active farming no longer appreciates the hurly burly of the race course and prefers to watch the action on television.

In a recent interview he said "I much prefer watching the big races at home on the television - you can get much closer to the action".

The last race that Tom Price saw Flakey Dove in live action was the Hoechst Panacur Mares Final at Newbury in 1991.

Little more than twelve months previously Flakey Dove had made her own racecourse debut in a modest bumper at Ludlow. She was backed in from 16/1 to tens, led seven furlongs out and as was to be expected from her pedigree held on gamely to win in a tight finish.

The filly did not appreciate the heavy going at Haydock next time but still ran well to finish runner up to Pamera in the hands of Jimmy Duggan's amateur rider brother Damian.

Two hours after Mr Frisk had won the Seagram Grand National Flakey Dove completed her ration of bumbers with a creditable second place behind Little Sail at Hereford, scene of so many brave displays by both her dam and grand-dam.

The Price family put on their thinking caps over the summer of 1990 and planned a spring campaign with the final of the Hoechst Panacur Mares Only series as their target.

Flakey Dove did not enjoy the happiest of hurdling debuts. She reappeared in a Hoechst Qualifier at Worcester in late February and fell at the second flight.

Debs Ball winning at Wetherby

The ill fated Blyton Lad

Lochsong with lad Chris Scudder.

Flakey Dove the Champion Hurdler.

The Jack Berry trained Luck Parkes winning at Chester.

The now retired Stack Rock winning at Chester.

Bobs Return wins the 1993 Great Voltigeur, at York, in great style.

Jodami and a smiling Mark Dwyer after winning the 1993 Cheltenham Gold cup.

Stack Rock and a delighted Sue Alston (left)

Mister Baileys becomes the first Northern trained Classic winner for a generation

Lochsong wins at Sandown with her jockey looking round for non existent dangers.

Majed, possibly the best dual purpose horse in training.

Antonin, the 1995 Cheltenham Gold Cup winner ?

A week later she completed the course in third place behind Springaleak and there then followed the first of the now familiar 'one-two' sequences.

Flakey Dove ran at Uttoxeter on Saturday 16th March - not particularly well either managing a distant fourth behind Truth Be Told. The very next Saturday she was back in action at Newbury with Dai Tegg on board in the final of the Hoechst Series and hacked up by twelve lengths from Church Leap.

'Led two out; soon clear', was the summary of the close up and in future seasons the habit of giving Flakey Dove a warm up race only a short period before her principal target has proved equally successful.

Within the Price 'think tank' it was now clear that the daughter of Shadey Dove had the potential to emulate her dam who herself had won nine races over timber.

As Flakey Dove's sire Oats had finished third in the Derby, the future was promising, though at this formative stage of her career, dreams of the Champion Hurdle had not become more than a fleeting thought in connections' minds.

1991-92 saw Flakey Dove enjoying a long spell out at grass. She was not brought into training until November and did not see the racecourse until February.

A first time out success over Dara Doone at Warwick presaged a most lucrative sequence of victories in handicap company. Flakey Dove scored popular wins at Doncaster, Ascot and Liverpool where she cruised into the lead at the final flight and accounted for Cheerful Times and Viking Flagship with stylish authority.

May Bank Holiday Monday saw the Prices at Haydock for the Swinton Hurdle. 11st 3lbs was a tall order for the mare but she didn't let them down.

Starting at 6/1 favourite she chased the leaders throughout and stayed on at her own pace to finish third beaten one length and four by Bitofabanter and Castle Secret.

Chasers and Hurdlers 1991-92 were fulsome in their praise. Their essayist wrote "One of the most improved handicappers of the season...won at Warwick in February off a mark of 96 and ended the season finishing third to Bitofabanter in the Swinton Handicap Hurdle off 127...idles once in front...best at two miles...will improve further."

A campaign aimed at the Smurfit Champion Hurdle was planned for 1992-93 but the strategy misfired. Flakey Dove was in season when finishing a modest fifth in the Tote Gold Trophy and despite gaining a comfortable success in Warwick's Regeney Hurdle could only finish seventh behind Granville Again at Cheltenham.

The suggestion at the time was that Flakey Dove filled the bill as a handicap hurdler but lacked the quality to compete on level terms with potential champion hurdlers.

With hindsight Richard Price was nearer the truth with his reflections after Flakey Dove had won the 1994 Cleeve Hurdle at Cheltenham.

He said "I was never really happy with her in 1992-93. She had a bit of a foot problem then but we found he answer to that and she's very well in herself now."

It has been said that Flakey Dove is a mare who trains herself on the racecourse; The theory is only partially true. She may well hone the cutting edges of her fitness on the track but Richard Price is too knowledgeable a stockman to let her race without a thorough preparation at home.

Prior to the 1993-94 National Hunt season Richard primed his mare with an outing on the flat at Nottingham. She won the extended fourteen furlong maiden with a degree of comfort and duly began her Cheltenham build up with a respectable fourth to the enigmatic Debs Ball in the Tote West Yorkshire Hurdle at Wetherby.

The outing was in the nature of a "blow out" as the distance of 3 miles 1 furlong was arguably beyond the mare's range of stamina. Competent rather than sparkling performances then followed at Ascot, in the Bula Hurdle at Cheltenham and at Windsor in the New Years Day Hurdle.

Flakey Dove returned to the winner's circle at Haydock's late January fixture. She slammed Tiananmen Square by twenty lengths in the Champion Hurdle Trial and a week later returned to Cheltenham to gain an equally impressive victory in The Leeve Hurdle.

Richard Dunwoody was in the saddle and the win provided the champion Jockey with the 1,000th success of ihs career.

Later that raw January afternoon Dunwoody elaborated on Flakey Dove. "She's a smashing mare and very tough. She will give someone a grand ride in the champion. She gave me a great feel at Haydock and she did the same today. She jumped super".

Thinking ahead to the Tote Gold Trophy, her trainer expressed the views that she should run a better race than she had in 1993 as the dates indicated that she would not be in season.

As many an unfortuante mother has discovered the calendar is not to be relied upon and Flakey Dove was "late".

In the event Flakey Dove was hard ridden approaching the final flight and took third place, beaten a short head and four lengths by Large Action and Oh So Risky.

Richard opted for one more race before Cheltenham. Flakey Dove returned to Newbury ten days before the Festival and won the Berkshire Hurdle by twenty lengths from Ivors Flutter.

The report in the Racing Post suggested that Flakey Dove "had consolidated her position as a live champion hurdle outsider".

The description was to prove a shade more accurate than George Ennor's assessment after the Tote Gold Trophy.

Commenting on the mare's defeat, George wrote "she was a brave third, four lengths back but her championship limitations were exposed".

George was justified in his caveat and no doubt he would have modified his words had he the benefit of the Berkshire Hurdle form at his disposal.

Despite the ease of her Newbury success, memories of Flakey Dove's defeat by both Oh So Risky and Large Action in the Tote Gold Trophy influenced the Champion Hurdle market.

Flakey Dove was allowed to start at 9/1. A video recording of the Smurfit Champion Hurdle will indicate that the mare was always travelling supremely easily. She made steady headway throughout the last mile to throw down a challenge at the final flight and come clear up the hill to win by 1½ lengths from Oh So Risky with Large Action ¾ of a length further adrift in third.

Yet another in the never ending sequence of 'David against Goliaith' Victories had been accomplished at the festival.

In a brilliant post mortem to the Champion Hurdle, Brough Scott described Flakey Dove as "This Plain Jane with a vengeance. Lean and hard and a fair bit of hair around the heel."

He also added as a postscript "that the formbook could tell you one thing but your eye knew another. He (Oh So Risky) wouldn't pass her if they ran all the way to Gloucester and beyond."

After Cheltenham Richard Price announced new objectives for Flakey Dove. Hurdling would be forgotten and a serious attack on the major 'Cup' races of the summer season would be on the agenda.

As a token effort Flakey Dove went to Aintree for The Martell Aintree Hurdle. She might just as well have remained at home. In hock deep ground the mare could never extract her hooves from the mire and finished an exhausted fifth, thirty three lengths behind Danoli, the new wonder horse form Ireland.

A week earlier Flakey Dove had opened her 1994 account on the flat with a cosy three and a half length win over Star Play er in the Cheadle Hulme Stakes at Haydock.

Dreams of Ascot Gold Cup fame were dashed later in the month. The sticky ground did not help but Flakey Dove trailed in a well beaten ninth behind Safety In Numbers in the Sagaro Stakes.

Always a realist, Richard Price made no excuses. Instead he turned the mare out to grass. Flakey Dove did well, she is back in training and will be campaigned in all the top hurdles, culminating in the defence of her title at Cheltenham in March.

"Flakey Dove has never looked better", adds her trainer who now concentrates on the horses full time, leaving the farming to "the other Prices".

"She comes from a late developing family and she really enjoys her racing. We're all looking forward to next Spring".

BOBS RETURN

"Like Master like Dog"; in my case only too true; both of us are self-indulgent and a shade on the obstinate side.

The old adage has rarely been applied to "trainer and horse" but in the case of Mark Tompkins and Bob's Return the comparison will certainly stand the test of time.

The compulsory huddle with the gentlemen of the press in the winner's circle does not appeal to a fair number of the training fraternity but no-one could be more open straight forward or helpful than the master of Flint Cottage. To say that his co-operation is down to his origins as a blunt free speaking Yorkshireman is not entirely true. Experience suggests that there are several trainers from that area who keep their plans notably close to their chests.

Bob's Return runs his races in the same way that Mark Tompkins conducts his post-race interviews. There are no short measures or reservations about the colts attitude to racing: no pernickety likes or dislikes about distance, ground conditions or the standard of the opposition.

Be it the St Leger, the Prix Ganay, The Coral-Eclipse or the King George, this honest, good topped, teak brown racehorse will knuckle down to the business in forth-right but uncomplaining fashion and give unstintingly of his best.

Not being a pedigree student but rather a follower of form on the race course I find it interesting that Bobs Return attracted such little interest from the influential 'image makers of the Turf' until his victory in the 1993 Coalite St Leger eventually forced the traditionalists into grudging approval of the classic winner "born the wrong side of the tracks".

As a two year old Bobs Return merited a rating of 99p. In Racehorses of 1992, his write up covered four lines, though in support of Timeform it should be pointed out that they described him "as a really progressive colt" and their subsequent essay on Bobs Return in the 1993 annual more than made up for their previous lack of enthusiasm.

It needs to be said however that the media and for that matter the whole race-going public were dilatory in their recognition of the colt's performances and all too ready to find disparaging reasons for his success.

Bobs Return tended to be regarded as 'fluke' winner of the Group 3 Lingfield Derby Trial-a race in any case that sadly appears to have lost its kudos over the past decade. The fact that Bobs Return finished 6th in the Ever Ready Derby was hit upon as an excuse to denigrate the form of the current crop of three year olds and even when the Tompkins star accounted for Foresee in the Group 2 Great Voltigeur Stakes at York with markedly more authority them Commander In Chief had managed in Ireland. The establishment dwelt on the paucity of his breeding rather than the outtstanding consistency of his achievements.

The St Leger triumph finally caused a re-think while subsequent running as a four year old has underlined his quality.

Mind you a solid faction still remain who regard Bobs Return Doncaster victory as an undervalued classic win on the grounds that the race itself non longer deserves its historic label as "The Oldest Classic."

They stress the steady decrease in entries, the comparative-
ly small fields on the day, the relative lack of star names
competing, and the pre-eminence of the Arc de Triumphe.

Thank goodness the Doncaster authorities have stood firm.
Those lucky enough to attend the St Leger Meeting over the
past few seasons cannot fail to have sampled the deep seated
fervour with which the Leger is still regarded by northerners,
while the management themselves are also to be warmly con-
gratulated on their efforts to maintain the high profile of the
race. Their stand has in the main been justified by the subsequent performances of recent St Leger winners and that of
Bobs Return who has done nothing to lower the standard.

Critics would do well to remember that the purpsoe of the St
Leger was to test the staying power of the top three year olds
in training. Stamina allied to speed remains an essential
characteristic in all outstanding thoroughbreds and the
Doncaster classic serves this purpose admirably.

The entry system has admittedly required an overhaul but
John Sanderson is too shrewd an administrator to overlook
this discrepancy and his decision to allow a later cut off point
for entry is to be applauded.

Mark Tompkins is on record as saying that he bought Bobs
Return on his physical potential as a racehorse rather than
on his admiration for the colts breeding.

The attitude is typical of the man and the rumour that Bobs
Return had been schooled over hurdles between the time he
had finished sixth at Epsom in the Derby and his return to
action at York also comes as no surprise.

Future seasons may prove Bob's Return to be the fore runner of a fashionable classic blood-line but at the time of his purchase at Goff's October Yearling sale, this was not overtly apparent. Bob Back, his sire was by Roberto, a stallion not renowned for his consistency while Quality Of Life, his dam, was a modest winner in Ireland as a two year old.

Bob Back is best remembered for his shock 33/1 defeat of Pebbles and Commanche Rum in the Prince of Wales Stakes at Royal Ascot.

At the end of his four year old campaign he was exported to race in the States where he started his career with a promising second in the Man O' War Stakes.

Sadly this excellent beginning was not maintained and Bob Back returned to stud in Ireland during 1988 having only scored one victory.

When Mark Tompkins purchased Bob's Return the success rate of his sire's initial crop did not suggest that a potential champion stallion was about to emerge on the scene.

One has to look back along "The bottom line" of the pedigree to discover latent quality. Narrow Escape, the great grandam of Bobs Return, was not only a half sister to Pushful but had herself won her first three races as a two year old, including The Chesham Stakes. Narrow Escape was by the Coronation Cup winner Narrator out of Press Forward the daughter of Precipitation and the winner of the Cheshire Oaks.

The breeding may not be "blue riband" material but it is eminently respectable.

Quality of Life was the property of John O'Connor, manager

of the Bally Linch Stud, the home of Bob Back. Bobs Return failed to attract any interest as a foal at Newmarket but was described by those at Bally Linch "as always looking the part - a smashing individual - typical of his father Bob Back". The same authorities however, never dreamt that they were looking at a future classic winner.

Though she would not admit it today, there must also be doubts about Jackie Smith's original confidence that the horse she was given as a 13th wedding anniversary present would defy 'The unlucky number' to such a dramatic extent.

Her husband George, the proprietor of a paper recycling business in Leicester, purchased Bobs Return off Mark Tompkins before the colt had opened his two year old account. The trainer himself had gone to £14,500 to buy the colt at Kill.

Before Bobs Return had lined up for this year's King George VI and Queen Elizabeth Diamond Stakes at Ascot in late July, the colt had won five of his twelve races and amassed prize money amounting to £383,287 - a tidy little profit for the Smith family who were making their first venture into racehorse ownership.

Bobs Return made his racecourse debut in the G.R.P. Massey Two Year Old Trophy at Beverley, a decent enough race if not considered a fashionable introductory race for potenial classic colts.

The colt had clearly shown ability at home. He started at 7/2 but "start" was not really the operative word. He flopped out of the stalls - something winners can never do at Beverley and despite making headway from the two furlong marker was not able to land a challenge.

Bobs Return was off the course for three months. When he reappeared at Yarmouth it was to finish 4th behind Racing Telegraph in a competitive maiden. Again there was significant support for him in the market. He went off at 9/4 favourite (from 5/1) and ran on stoutly to finish fourth.

Losses were retrieved at Pontefract on October 22. This time Bobs Return was merely nibbled at in the ring but made it third time lucky at odds of 12/1. The formbook read "with leader led over one furlong out, stayed on Well."

Pontefract is a demanding course for a two year old and success over a mile at the West Yorkshire venue is a solid yardstick to suggest that ten furlongs at Newmarket will be well within reach.

The Sporting Life Zetland Stakes has proved an excellent guide for potential stars. Rock Hopper took the prize in 1989; Bonny Scot in 1991 and great hopes were held of Double Trigger when he landed the prize in 1993.

Bob's Return went off at 14/1 and made virtually every yard of the running. He accounted for Bobbie Dee and Sharjah by three quarters of a length and two and a half lengths.

The Smiths and their trainer returned to winter quarters confident that they had indeed secured a bargain.

Not the least of Mark Tompkins' qualities as a trainer is his ability "to have a horse right" first time out and Bob's Return was turned out a picture for the Lingfield Derby Trial.

Starting at 14/1 he again made all the running and only needed to be pushed out to beat Tiomaw Island and Shareek. Azzilfi, later fancied to reverse the placings in the St Leger was a well beaten fourth. On the strength of this win Bobs

Return was touted as an attractive outsider for the Ever Ready Derby. He had handled the hill nicely at Lingfield and his stamina was unquestioned.

In the event the colt finished sixth after racing in the van until rounding Tattenham Corner.

Philip Robinson, his regular jockey, explained that he had floundered in the rain softened and well watered ground in the home straight.

Philip added "he was all over the shop when he hit the soft patches."

It was to be this apparent dislike of soft ground that was to cause the supporters more than a little anxiety when the heavens opened at Doncaster only three days before the St Leger.

Before that however, Bobs Return was to underline his quality with a runaway six lengths win from Foresee in the Great Voltigeur at York.

The colt looked splendid in the preliminaries and could be named the winner from a long way out.

Breeding pundits still expressed their doubts but the leading bookmakers took a more positive view. They promoted Bobs Return 3/1 favourite for the Coalite St Leger and despite the fears of a soft surface, they were proved handsomely correct.

Jockey, Philip Robinson was also "spot on" when he predicted that Bobs Return would be equally effective ridden from mid-division as he had been from the front in previous races.

Bobs Return did pull for his head early on but he consented

to be settled in third place and it was not until approaching the three furlong marker that Robinson asked him to quicken.

The response was immediate and Bobs Return had his race won in a matter of strides. He returned to a standing ovation from a patriotic northern crowd who had adopted the horse and his connections as their own.

Victory was as emotional experience both for the Sheffield born Tompkins who had watched Nijinsky win the St Leger from the rails at the age of 19 and for owner Jackie Smith, whose father had worked 'down the mines' at nearby Harworth Colliery.

Bobs Return ended his three year old campaign with an honourable sixth to Urban Sea in the Ciga Prix de L' Arc de Triomphe, beaten about four lengths.

Mark Tompkins' belief that his horse would improve further as a four year old has been amply justified even if the colt has yet to gain outright success.

Bobs Return had little chance of winning the Prix Ganay over an inadequate trip in softish ground but was not disgraced in finishing fourth.

Heavily backed to retrieve his reputation in the Hardwicke stakes at Royal Ascot, he failed by a neck to overhaul Bobzao, after seeing the winner on the home turn.

Attacking tactics were then employed as Sandown in the Coral-Eclipse where he led at a furious pace for a mile and kept on in courageous style to fill the runners up berth one and a half lengths behind Ezzoud with a host of top horses in arrears.

Bobs Returns was thought to be at a disadvantage racing right handed but the Eclipse proved otherwise. His subsequent dissapointing run in the King George, at right handed Ascot can partly be excused because the loose horse Ezzoud, who had unshipped Walter Swinburn, acted as a lead for Bobs Return and he set a fantastic gallop until being overhauled in the straight.

Further poor performances at York and in the Irish St Leger have followed. His connections may well be pondering his future, but whether he stays in training or goes off to enjoy stallion duties - one thing is sure he was one of the bargain buys of recent times.

CASTLEREA LAD

Castlerea Lad cost 3800 Irish punts as a yearling and four seasons later his prize money tally stands at £42,470.

Even if the Reg Hollinshead trained five year old were to retire from racing at this moment he would have been a bargain but he should have at least three more seasons ahead of him and if his past consistency is any guide, the son of Efisio is certain to land a valuable sprint handicap before he loses his biting edge.

Reg Hollinshead has always held a high regard for Castlerea Lad. Unlike many of his less talented stable companions he has averaged only nine races per season, winning six times and being placed on five other occasions.

The record might not seem unusual but the Hollinshead horses are kept busier than most as a glance at 'the trainers' statistics would indicate. On September 20th the yard had notched 28 winners from no less than 343 runners - a strike rate of 6%.

Only five trainers in Britain, Messrs Hannon, Berry, Cole, Johnston and Channan had raced a larger number of horses during the current season.

Far from being a criticism the figures are in effect a recommendation. Reg Hollinshead has been in the business long enough to know that moderate horses, once fit, need to be raced regularly in order to make the best use of their opportunities. The better the horse, the more demanding the job becomes and by inference the greater the need for a rest between races.

At the age of 70, Reg Hollinshead has lost none of his appetite for racing. He still drives hundreds of miles a day to watch his horses in action and to return in plenty of time to deal with any emergencies at home and supervise morning work the next day. Overnight stays are few and far between and even now Reg prefers to drive to a course like Hamilton Park, watch the racing, go back home and repeat the performance all over again the following day rather than book himself into a hotel.

Reg has been training horses professionally since 1951. Before that he had ridden with consistent success over the jumps. He prepared his first winner as a permit holder in the 1948-49 season and also holds the distinction of partnering the last two winners ever recorded at the long defunct Woore racecourse.

Reg has trained will over 1300 winners in the 43 years that he has held a professional licence and passed the 1,000 winner mark on the flat at Chester in May. Over the past five years he has averaged 42 winners per season but punters still find him a hard man to follow.

It is simply the case that Reg's horses race so frequently and at such a variety of courses, that if the race-goer has not actually watched their progress from the stands with his or her own eyes, the task of 'catching the right day' is indeed a demanding test.

The Hollinshead stable is frequently described as "The Rugeley academy for young riders" - a label that has been gained over the years by the unparalleled success that Reg has enjoyed in educating young apprentices.

Many household names owe their positions to the instruction they first received from Reg.

Walter Swinburn, Kevin Darley, Steve Perks, Willie Ryan, Tony Culhane and Gary Hind to mention but half a dozen are all ex-Hollinshead apprentices and come to think of it, the necessity to give them all race riding experience is one of the reasons why the Hollinshead horses are so rarely wasting their time standing idle in their boxes.

Castlerea Lad's record marks him down as a horse 'above the salt' in the Hollinshead stable, a distinction that the trainer himself underlined when the bay was beginning his career as a three year old.

He runs in the colours of Tessa Graham whose husband Jim has had horses at Rugeley for many years - and here it should be stressed that Reg Hollinshead has commanded a loyal following from the same pool of owners over a long period of time - in itself a sure recommendation for any trainer.

The Grahams also owned Nominator who only cost 5,200 guineas as a yearling, but went on to crown his two year old career with victory in the Somerville Tattersall Stakes before running with much credit both in the Craven Stakes and the 1993, 2,000 Guineas.

Nominator was sold for a very substantial five figure sum to race in America and the owners have had to turn down a number of tempting offers for Castlerea Lad.

As a two year old he raced six times and was never out of the first four, winning a maiden auction event at Pontefract and after an absence of three months being placed in nurseries at Haydock and Doncaster.

The impression that Castlerea Lad would improve as a three year old was endorsed when he scored over six furlongs at Haydock in May. The race was the Be Friendly Handicap and Castlerea Lad stuck on gamely to defy the persistent challenge of Linda Perratt's Petite d'Argent.

I remember Reg Hollinshead beaming with pleasure and indicating to the listening press that this was an improving sort who would win more races.

Castlerea Lad won a claimer at the Merseyside track in August but he needed another year to develop his potential.

The colt also required a sound surface to reveal his true ability. The 1993 spring was wet and conditions were against Castlerea Lad when he made his first two appearances behind Gorinsky at Doncaster and Ripon.

The ground had firmed up for the Guineas meeting at Newmarket and Castlerea Lad, starting at 10/1, quickened decisively from the dip to beat Martinosky and Troon, a shade cleverly.

The close up read "held up; headway to lead inside the final furlong ran on."

Tessa Graham, who has enjoyed enormous pleasure from watching her colours being carried for the first time, confirms that this is the way her horse likes to race.

"He seems to prefer it", she agrees. "Most of his jockeys try to keep him handy and then ask him to go on and win his race from the furlong marker. Willie Ryan always knows the right moment to pop the question though Willie Carson and Frankie Dettori have been equally good".

Reg Hollinshead was himself responsible for buying Castlerea Lad as a yearling but Tessa Graham proved her ability as a shrewd judge of horses by picking him out on looks.

"I just liked his attitude", she said "and the staff at the stable have always had the same opinion. They love his laid back ways and call him 'Cassy'."

The Grahams live on the Clwyd - Cheshire border and are starting to breed their own stock. They do not have a resident stallion but are hoping that Castlerea Lad will fill the gap when he finally retires from racing.

Tessa Graham also owns an unraced two year old called Roscommon Lad of whom she has high hopes.

Castlerea Lad used to be something of a pernickety feeder and as a two year old it was a problem to get him to put on condition.

The difficulty disappeared in dramatic fashion - Castlerea Lad and a couple of his colleagues were contentedly exercising in the horse-walker when 'the electrics' short circuited and 'the arms' of the walker became live.

Castlerea Lad's companions were both electrocuted but by miraculous off chance Cassy himself escaped unscathed.

From that day onwards it was as if he realised that life was worth the effort. His appetite increased. He put on condition and his work rate on the race course has been beyond criticism.

In 1993 Caltlerea Lad went on to complete a hat trick with victories in the Citroen Xantia Sprint at Goodwood and the Wynyad Classic Northumberland Sprint Trophy at Newcastle.

The latter occasion coincided with the visit of the Queen to watch the centenary of the Northumberland Plate and Castlerea Lad landed "a royal touch" being backed down from 8/1 to 9/2 and justifying the confidence with a comfortable two length success over Educated Pat with Farfelu a length adrift in third place.

Once again the close up noted his smooth headway to lead inside the final furlong and his ability to run on well.

Six days later Castlerea Lad attempted the near impossible by trying to give away 8lbs to John Gosden's Catrail in the Pennine Stakes at Haydock. Subsequent events have shown what a difficult task, the Graham's sprinter was being asked to undertake. He made a brave effort to close on the Newmarket trained favourite but was fighting a losing battle from the furlong market.

Catrail went on to win by six lengths but connections were delighted with Castlerea Lad's efforts and he headed for Goodwood as a 14/1 chance for the Vodac Stewards Cup.

"He never got into the race at all," recalls the owner. "We had been very hopeful but he was outpaced all the way. Perhaps it was the big field and the jostling for position that upset him but Willie (Ryan) reported that he was never happy."

Castlerea Lad finished 21st out of 29 runners and he was given six weeks to recover. The 5 furlongs and 140 yards of the Tote Portland stakes proved too sharp for the

Hollinshead contender. He made late headway but could do no better than eleventh, ten lengths adrift of the winner.

"He raced once more," adds Tessa Graham. "We started him in the Ladbrokes Ayr Gold Cup and he ran a great race from a dreadful draw."

In fact Castlerea Lad came home first of the group who raced on the stands side and amply vindicated the expenses of the journey.

"He has yet to win as a five year old," continues Tessa, "but the handicapper has not been kind."

Newmarket's Guineas Meeting saw Castlerea Lad finish fifth to Double Blue at level weights. He was beaten two and a half lengths.

At York's May meeting the four year old came too late off the pace and finished 4th to Roger The Butler, Double Blue and Poker Chip - 'headway final furlong - stayed on.'

On the strength of these two creditable runs, Reg upped the distance to 7 furlongs for Castlerea Lad's next outing at Doncaster.

The Keepmoat Holdings Handicap saw Castlerea Lad make his effort three furlongs out but over the extra furlong he could make no further improvement.

"Definitely not one of his 'going days'," she admits.

By now Reg Hollinshead was aiming for the Wokingham with a warm up race scheduled for Pontefraet.

Frankie Dettori had the mount Castlerea Lad carried top

weight of 9st 10lbs and was a usual 'held up, made headway 2 furlongs out kept on under pressure'.

He finished sixth beaten less than two lengths by Two Moves In Front. Castlerea Lad returned home in a subdued manner. The following weekend he was heard to cough. He was among the first, as Reg Hollinshead remembers well.

"We had a virus doing the rounds and Castlerea Lad was one of the first to suffer."

He was scratched from the Wokingham and forced to take matters easily.

Castlerea Lad was never seriously ill but the decision not to run was eminently sensible. He has been working well at Rugeley and the Grahams are hopeful.

Whatever happens at Goodwood there are a series of Autumn handicaps in which Castlerea Lad can play a leading role.

The final word comes from Tessa Graham - "I'm not that keen on Goodwood even though he's won there last year. I think he needs a wider course. It's a pity but our local track at Chester is right out, the turns are much too tight."

RIVER NORTH

Peter Savill and Lady Herries make an unlikely couple - the one admitting that if he didn't bet, his annual racing liabilities would amount to around £400,000 the other, married to Colin Cowdrey and a daughter of the late Duke of Norfolk born with the proverbial silverspoon in her mouth and thankfully free from the need to wager to cover her costs.

- A pair of opposites if ever there was one but there you would be unequivocally mistaken. Owner and trainer are united in their passion for the sport of racing and both regard the other with a high degree of mutual respect.

Peter Savill's self disciplined pragmatic approach to the betting side of the business and his insiders knowledge of where best to place his horses is ideally complimented by Lady Herries' natural flair to instill her horses with that special brand of confidence which enables them to reproduce their best form when it is most required.

Add to that inherent quality some of the finest gallops in the country, a loyal highly experienced stable staff plus the invaluable assistance of her step-daughter in law Maxine Cowdrey and it is no surprise that Peter Savill's maroon and light blue colours are now a familiar sight in the tack room at Angmering Park.

Maxine played a significant role in the purchase of River North. She had noted the colt at Freemason Lodge while riding out for Michael Stoute and recommended his purchase at the 1992 Newmarket Autumn sales.

River North had only run once in public for the Stoute stable, on heavy ground in a back end 6 furlong maiden at Folkestone. Eleven runners had gone to post. River North looked a shade backward. Ridden by Paul Eddery he started an easy 5/1 chance, made a forward move at the half way stage but came under pressure below the distance and stayed on at one pace to finish third behind the 11/8 favourite Semillon.

Lady Herries had raced her husband's Dawn Flight at the meeting. She was happy with what she had seen and within the fortnight River North was safely in his box at Littlehampton.

The half brother to the winning miler Ante Ua, had cost 21,000 guineas as a yearling but was knocked down to Lady Herries for a third of the price.

At 7000 guineas River North has emerged as one of the bargains of the decade. Within one and a half seasons his prize money tally stands at £137,367. He has won 5 races and finished a close second in three other valuable events.

River North, a gelding, remains only four years old. He will have at least three more full seasons ahead of him and has already shown the ability to win in Group 3 company .

Campaigned abroad River North will surely be capable of winning in Group 2 even possibly Group 1 company.

He has no future value as a stallion so will be trained with success on the track as the sole objective.

His success in 1993 led to Peter Savill investing in another two horses at Angmering Park. Both these two year olds, Arctic Thunder and Celtic Swing gained impressive victories at Ayr's two day mid-July meeting and Celtic Swing won in such exciting style that his owner predicted success at the highest level.

Peter Savill finished tenth in the 1993 owners' list amassing over £221,772 in winning prize money. He won 52 races, one short of his best ever score which would have been equalled if River North himself had not been disqualified for failing a dope test at Brighton.

No - there wasn't any suggestion of foul play; merely an unfortunate association with one of the Herries' hounds. The dog had been under treatment from antibiotics and had rather rudely raised his leg over a batch of hay which was then consumed by River North who in turn revealed traces of the offending medication in his urine at the time of the test - at least Peter Easterby's No Bombs had had the pleasure of eating a Mars Bar before his demotion in similar circumstances at Worcester!

Peter Savill is careful to spread his fifty plus team of horses over some twenty different trainers. This all encompassing catchment area provides him with many diverse advantages. First of all he can send suitable horses to suitable trainers.

Late two year olds to stables who specialize in that category, precocious juveniles to those whose record is contrastingly good with the sharp early sorts, middle distance horses to trainers who produce their best results with that type and stayers and potential hurdlers to the likes of Mary Reveley or Peter Easterby.

Then the wider the net, the greater the information and not

the least is the in built safety valve that the system provides against the spread of the virus. The owner avoids the pit fall of putting too many eggs in one basket and seeing all his horses catch the cough at one fell swoop.

River North was gelded soon after his arrival at Lady Herries' stable. He had most of the winter to recover from the shock and made his first appearance of the 1993 season at Doncaster on William Hill Lincoln day.

River North finished third behind Majority, making late headway in the hands of Kevin Darley, Peter Savill's retained rider.

The publisher turned chartered submarine provider for the tourist and exploration industry in the Caribbean had been made aware of River North's promise and required his jockey to rubber stamp the purchase.

Next time out at Brighton, River North exchanged Lady Herries' sky blue and red for Peter Savill's familiar maroon and light blue; jacket sent off a well-backed 9/4 second favourite, the gelding won by a clever half length from conspicuous and the Gosden hot pot Kinema Red.

Ripon was the next stop for River North who caused knowledgeable race - readers to stretch for their notebooks when he quickened readily in the closing stages to account for Julie Cecil's Rapid Repeat by a comfortable three and a half lengths.

This was a Class B 0-95 handicap and River North was always travelling on the bridle.

The 3 year old was returned at 11/4 and the money was down in confident style when he reappeared in the Zetland Gold

Cup at Redcar.

River North was supported from 5/2 to 15/8 favourite with at least one major bet of £24,000 to £12,000 being recorded.

Once again Kevin Darley was able to drop him in behind before making use of his substantial turn of foot to hit the front inside the last furlong and outpace the useful Philidor by a length.

River North's emerging quality was confirmed on Timeform Charity Day at York, where he cruised home hard held to beat Jackpot Star and Key to My Heart.

I say "hard held" but with hindsight the winner did betray signs of idling in front, a characteristic that has influenced Kevin Darley in all his subsequent races.

Darley has matured into the North's finest jockey since the hey-days of Edward Hide. An excellent judge of pace he is a natural horseman and a most powerful finisher. Furthermore he is an intelligent and communicative personality who can be relied upon to provide connections with accurate and informative advice on all the horses he rides.

Darley and Peter Savill are a fine team and punters have not been slow to appreciate their worth.

The mid-summer target for River North had always been the £80,000 Royal Hong Kong Jockey Club Trophy at Sandown. A big field contained experienced handicappers of the ilk of Philidor, Show Faith and Wainwright.

River North and Smarginato were the two three year olds with outstanding winning form since the weights were published. They dominated the contest with John Dunlop's

Smarginato proving the stronger up the final hill to prevail by one and a half lengths.

River North, who had hardened from early fours down to 3/1 favourite, was backed to take £40,000 out of the ring. Some critics suggested that River North was "over the top" at Sandown but he was carried wide on the home turn and had the misfortune to come up against an improving rival who produced his best on the day.

Now fully exposed, River North's future had to lie in Pattern Company, Peter Savill has always been a major player on and a much appreciated supporter of the Scottish circuit.

It came as little surprise then to find River North among the acceptors for the Tennents Scottish Classic at Ayr.

Kevin Darley was seen at his tactical best in this Group 3 event, taking the initiative to drive for home between the final two furlongs and having enough in reserve to ease down near the line and still hold Only Royale by three quarters of a length.

River North's win was extremely popular with Scottish race-goers.

The geldings attention was now focused on mainland Europe. He flew to Hoppegarten for a Group 3 event and was not discredited when third to Kornado and Lando, Germany's top three year olds.

If there was a disappointment for River North's supporters, it came at Goodwood in September.

As Kevin Darley later said "I thought that he had progressed so well through the season that he would be able to take

Knifebox but he did not produce the anticipated turn of foot and the favourite stuck on gamely to score."

The reason was not too hard to find. River North was suffering from a hair-line fracture of the splint bone and continued to be affected by splint trouble on both forelegs during the winter.

Plans to campaign him on the softish ground in the spring had to be shelved and Lady Herries opted to aim River North at the Hardwicke Stakes.

His training programme proceeded better than anticipated and the four year old was given a preparatory warm up in a listed race at Leicester.

River North delighted connections with a promising second to Mack The Knife but blazing sunshine at Ascot dried out the ground and it was unanimously decided to abort the pre-arranged plan.

Much to the pleasure of the Savill camp, thunderstorms deluged the course on the final day of the July meeting at Newmarket and River North gained clear-cut revenge over his old enemy Mack The Knife to win the Fred Archer Stakes a shade cleverly.

There was very little pace on during the early stages and River North found himself having to put in two spurts to win his race. Quickening twice he scored in decisive fashion despite hanging left handed under pressure.

River North's next race was a second attempt at the Tennents Scottish Classic.

Ground conditions appeared ideal until a drying wind and

hot sunshine combined to turn good going into a near firm surface by the time of the race.

Lady Herries, Peter Savill and Kevin Darley all hesitated before finally giving the go-ahead to run. River North appeared heavily bandaged on both forelegs. He was drawn on the wide outside and as is his wont was held up towards the rear as the field turned for home.

Darley still had some ten lengths to find approaching the two furlong maker when Michael Hills set Beneficial alight in front and at the same moment River North was momentarily hampered.

In the circumstances he achieved a small miracle to get within a short head of Beneficial on the line. The loss was expensive for Peter Savill, who remarked "The trip too short, the ground too fast but he still should have won."

It was an accurate summary but don't blame Darley. He was in the classic Catch 22 situation. He had to look after his horse on the fast going and at the same time give him every chance to win.

Had he not been checked by a beaten horse drifting off time a true line approaching the final furlong the places of the first two would surely have been reversed.

Sadly for his backers, it was not to be, particularly that bold punter who stalked £6000 to win £21,000 and saw it disappear by the shortest of heads.

With suitable opportunities thin on the ground in Britain, River North's next race was the Group 1 Aral-Pokal at Gelsenkirchen-Horst. Starting at 6/1 in a field of six, River North was ridden to lead between the last two furlongs and under a hands and heels ride from Kevin Darley lengthened impressively to put the result beyond doubt.

River North beat Germany's top 4 year old Monsun by 2½ lengths with Snurge six lengths back in third place.

A delighted Lady Herries announced that River North improved by 7lbs every time he ran.

The gelding was expected to return to Germany for the Grosser Preis Von Baden on September 4th but was reported to have burst a blood vessel after his Aral-Pokal race and was forced to miss the race.

River North was returned to Cologne for a Group 1 race in September. He was unsuited by the slow early pace and finished well beaten. He may well run in Canada, mid October in his search for more group honours.

JODAMI

My eldest son is getting married before Christmas. The wedding arrangements have tended to cramp his racing style, something of a sadness at Budden Towers because he is a steadying influence on the purse strings.

'J.N.C' is also a shrewd punter with an innate capacity to pick out antepost value and first time out winners. At the age of 14 he visited the Grand National and told me to back Lucius. More recently we met on the roof of that wonderful old stand at Kelso shortly before the start of a modest bumper. It was back in the spring of 1990. Anyway, the horse mentioned was an animal called Jodami - "marvellous looking horse," confided James, "easily the pick of the paddock and the Beaumonts seem very chipper. I hope you've taken a bit of the 33's."

Needless to say Budden Senior had attempted 'to get out' on Shuttle Hill, the favourite trained by Tom Tate for whose horses I have always 'enjoyed' a fond weakness.

Prospects of victory were not improved when the five year old unseated his rider on the way to the start but going into the bottom bend. Shuttle Hill began to sprout wings and spirits rose until 'The bins' suddenly picked out the leader - a powerful deep chested dark bay with a long raking stride that was covering double the ground that Shuttle Hill could manage and had not been asked a question.

Even before I had picked out the familiar crouch of Anthea Farell - a quiet voice murmured beside me "bad luck, father Jodami's got it in the bag."

Indeed he had. Shuttle Hill quickly surrendered and though both One For The North and Mudahim never capitulated, the Beaumonts new acquisition from Ireland galloped home unchallenged to win by seven lengths.

Close inspection in the winners circle confirmed the suspicions earlier aroused by J.N.C.'s remarks. Jodami was indeed some horse - only five years old but already mature enough to go chasing - a natural steeplechaser if ever I saw one.

The affable Beaumonts could hardly restrain their delight. They had previously trained point to pointers for John Yeadon but it was only since Peter Beaumont had opted to take out a professional licence that the owners interest had been revived.

He had paid 25,000 guineas for the grey Choctaw and the latter's relatively modest success had whetted the appetite.

Yeadon is reported to have ordered his trainer to find "a real cracker jack" and Beaumont's son in law Patrick Farrell, whose Irish connections had ferreted out previous bargains for the stable, discovered Jodami shortly after he had been sold at the Tattersalls Derby Sale for 1R 12 500 guineas.

£16,000 was reputed to be the asking price and Peter Beaumont was offered upwards of five times that sum to part with the horse even before he had jumped a fence in public.

Jodami's immediate family may be little out of the ordinary but a more detailed check reveals close connections with the very best of Irish jumping blood. Equally important to the Beaumonts was the geldings physical make up. He looked the part, plenty of chest room, deep girthed yet athletic and powerful behind. Jodami also exuded that special 'presence' factor that is so often part and parcel of a star chaser.

His sire Crash Course, now alas deceased, has been responsible for a long line of successful staying chasers, notably Maid of Money, the Irish National winner, Captain Dibble, and Toby Balding's Romany King.

Jodami's dam Mastertown Lucy was herself unraced but is a full sister to the winning chaser Hurry Up Henry and a half sister to the useful Rugged Lucy.

Jodami also has a year younger full sister called Crashtown Lucy who has been successful both between the flags and under rules in Ireland.

Further research through the distaff side of Jodami's pedigree reveals a relationship with both the Cambridgshire runner up Dance All Night and the Lockinge winner Scottish Reel, while both his dam and grand-dam were sired by top jumping stallions, Bargello and Master Owen..

The closer one looks the classier Jodami becomes both in physique and in ancestral background.

The 33/1 may have been missed at Kelso but from that brisk afternoon in the Scottish borders to the sunshine of the afternoon at Cheltenham last March when Jodami was out-pointed by The Fellow, loyalty to the Brandsby chaser has been unswerving.

For a horse who was bought with steeplechasing specifically in mind, Jodami proved remarkably versatile both in bumpers and over hurdles.

Little more than a fortnight after his winning debut at Kelso, he contested the Seagram Supreme National Hunt Flat Race at Aintree. Critics of these bumper races allege that they are rarely contested by horses of any real class. The Seagram was an obvious exception. In addition to Jodami the race included horses of the calibre of Ruling, Minorettes Girl, Norman Conqueror and Mayfair Minx.

Hopes of regaining The Kelso losses were dashed when Jodami, a 16/1 chance, was hampered by a badly slipping saddle. Outpaced on the bottom turn he stayed on to finish a close fifth of 20.

Jodami fared better in the Doncaster Bloodstock Sales 'Supreme' N.H. Flat race at The Scottish National. He finished runner up to Ruling with the remainder well-beaten.

The 1990-91 season saw Jodami run six times over hurdles, winning five and finishing second to Robert Dear over the minimum distance at Wetherby in February.

He had opened his account by winning a twenty three runner novice hurdle at Nottingham in late January. Starting at a generous 10/1 and partnered for the first time by Patrick Farrell he led three out, was headed by Fouz, the favourite at the final flight but fought back tigerishly to regain the lead on the flat.

Defeat at Wetherby was followed by his first appearance over 2½ miles. Jodami went off at 5/4 joint favourite with Intrepid Lass and was driven out to win by one and a half lengths with the third horse twenty lengths adrift. Four days before the 1991 Cheltenham Festival Jodami scored again at Ayr accounting for Greystoke's, Another Dyer by a comfortable four lengths. This was another excellent performance and it left Gordon Richards in no doubts about the promise of the winner.

"That must be a nailing good horse," said Richards after the race. "I rate mine and he never got a look in."

Jodami consolidated his reputation at Wetherby on Easter Monday. He carried twelve stone and successfully conceded upwards of two stone to his nearest five rivals.

The Beaumont's pride and joy reserved his best performance for the well contested Scottish Farm Dairy Foods Novices Handicap Hurdle at Ayr's Scottish National meeting. Shannon Glen, who had won the Mumm Prize Novices Hurdle at Aintree headed the market but Jodami at 5/1 slammed the opposition by twelve lengths, leaving all those present convinced that they had been watching a future Cheltenham Festival winner.

Peter Beaumont has 'patience' written all over him. Everything from his guarded manner of speech, through his deliberate style of walking to the careful placing of his horses suggests a man of infinite patience and so it proved with Jodami's transition to fences.

The Crash Course gelding was at the top of every jumping Annual's 'Chasers to follow' for the 1991-92 season and Peter had been forced to put up 'The not for sale at any price' signs even before he had jumped a single fence in public. The essayist in the 1991-92 edition of Timeform's Chasers and Hurdlers produced an accurate smile when he remarked that "Jodami's first appearance in a novice chase at Kelso in mid - November attracted as great an amount of media attention as Graeme Hick's arrival at the crease in his first test against the West Indies earlier in the year."

The pressure was all the more intense as Patrick Farrell was injured and his wife Anthea was entrusted with the ride.

In these early efforts over fences the instructions seemed to be along the lines of "Jodami is a natural jumper - see a stride and let him have his head."

I stress this is only a personal impression and I have not consulted the Beaumonts on its accuracy but that is what it looked like from the stands.

Left in the main to his own devices his jumping was erratic - a cocktail of brilliant leaps interspersed with several 'hit or miss' attempts when he either got in too close or over-jumped. Jodami won his first three races over fences but was never foot perfect. The fact that he was still able to beat a horse of Kings Curate's standing by three lengths in the West of Scotland Pattern Novices Chase at Ayr, spoke volumes for his potential.

The Reynoldstown Novices Chase had proved the undoing of Carrick Hill Lad in 1991. Twelve months later it led to Jodami's initial defeat as a novice chaser.

Faced by only two rivals Jodami was forced to do all his own donkey work and in truth the stiff fences found him out. He never cleared them with any fluency and his lack of confidence led to a patchy display from his rider. Patrick Farrell had done the bulk of Jodami's schooling at home but here at Ascot he appeared unable to provide his mount with that vital quality of positive guidance when it was most needed. Having said this one must qualify the criticism by stressing the difficulty that Patrick was facing.

Michael Dickinson always maintained that the Ascot fences

would find out all but the most disciplined of jumpers and at this early stage of his chasing career Jodami was still deficient in this direction.

It was back to the drawing board. A niggling back injury also caused Jodami to miss Cheltenham.

He reappeared in the Mumm Mildmay Novices Chase at Liverpool. His jumping was almost foot perfect (he made one serious error at the fourth fence) and approaching the final obstacle he appeared set for victory only to be caught close home by Bradbury Star.

This run restored Jodami's reputation and on his last outing of the season he again advertised his latent talent.

Sent to Punchestown for the Woodchester Bank Gold Cup, he lay close to the leaders throughout but failed to quicken in the home straight and had to be content with third place behind Second Schedual.

Jodami jumped round Punchestown like an old hand. He was beaten four and a half lengths and it has to be said that he gave away at least three times this deficit by giving up the outside to nobody. The tactics were no doubt adopted to ensure that Jodami obtained the clearest possible view of the fences. In the short term they might have cost him outright victory at Punchestown but in the long term they provided the very experience that Jodami most required.

The bay was now ready for more demanding tasks. During the summer of 1992 an important decision was reached; one that was to have a far-reaching effect and one that caused the writer to break a lifetime's habit of caution and invest on Jodami at 20/1 to win the Cheltenham Gold Cup on the strength of his seasonal debut at Haydock in November.

The decision was to book Mark Dwyer to ride Jodami in all his races. The partnership clicked immediately and it's no disrespect to Patrick Farrell to say that Dwyer's presence in the saddle led to a small but crucial difference. Patrick, probably with the approval of his father in law, had appeared to leave much of the decision making to Jodami himself. Mark on the other hand applied positive direction from the saddle and the results were there for all to see when the partnership made their seasonal debut in the Edward Hanmer Memorial Chase at Haydock.

Jodami was beaten by Run For Free but defeat was solely caused by lack of 'match fitness'. The horse's jumping was a revelation.

Jodami looked a handicap certainty for the Hennessy but in the event he had to be content with the runners up berth behind Sibton Abbey. The placings might well have been reversed had Mark Dwyer set about Jodami in the manner that Adrian Maguire adopted on the winner.

Sibton Abbey was driven for all he was worth from between the last two fences and kept responding to his rider's demanding calls to retain the advantage right up to the line. In contrast Jodami was given a sympathetic ride and his Jockey's patient horsemanship was to reap its own reward later in the season.

Jodami was now fully fit for the first time and won the Mandarin Chase in workmanlike style. He then reversed previous Haydock form by accounting for Run For Free in the Peter Marsh Chase and crossed to Ireland to scrape home from Chatam in the Hennessy Cognac Gold Cup.

Bookmakers promoted the Yorkshire hero to 4/1 second

favourite for the Gold Cup but anxiety was expressed about Jodami's ability to act on fast ground and in face of the sustained markets support for The Fellow, John Yeadon's champion started at double the price on the day.

Jodami made a mockery of these pre-race worries about the sound surface. Stretching out in confident manner he measured the Cheltenham fences with that mixture of boldness and accuracy which is the hallmark of quality. Running downhill for the final time he accelerated smoothly to tackle the long time leader, Rushing Wild and arousing triumphant cheer swelled in the throats of all loyal northern racegoers as Mark Dwyer was seen to look round for dangers when the pair galloped as one towards the last fence.

Dwyer exuded confidence, allowing Rushing Wild to marginally jump ahead before asking Jodami to go about his business. The race was over in a couple of strides. Jodami quickened. Rushing Wild could only stay on at one pace and Dwyer could afford to ease his mount down close home.

A famous victory had been achieved and provided that the Beaumonts could keep Jodami in the peak of condition a repeat success in 1994 was more than a possibility.

This was to prove a crunch question in the run up to Cheltenham but earlier events were sufficient to prove that Jodami's long summer break had erased any unpleasant memories that the gelding might have harboured after his gruelling experience in the cauldron that is Cheltenham on Gold Cup day.

His supporters were shocked when he fell on his seasonal reappearance at Wetherby but they were back in good voice when he exacted revenge from Cab On Target in the Edward Hammer Memorial at Haydock.

Jodami started 2/7 for the rehearsal chase at Chepstow but throughout the last half mile he was labouring some way off the leading pair. He had to be shaken up to take second place at the fourteenth and had it all to do behind Party Politics when he hardly rose at the third last and blundered his way out of contention.

Jodami was reduced to a hapless half canter as he reached the post beaten five lengths and twelve.

The exhibition was too awful to be true. The question of drugs was upper most in a lot of minds, but the Beaumont horses then subsided in a mass vote of sympathy and the stable closed down for over a month.

Jodami was patently short of hard racing work when he returned to the course for the Peter Marsh Chase at Haydock.

Dwyer concentrated on an educational round but Jodami's enthusiasm had not been blunted by the pre-Christmas disaster at Chepstow. He jumped soundly and after being initially tapped for toe between the last two fences stayed on in determined fashion to finish best of all in third place beaten a head and two lengths by Zeta's Lad and Run For Free.

The Beaumonts' plan for a second Gold Cup triumph now entailed a return visit to Leopardstown for the Hennessy Cognac Gold Cup. 1993 had seen Jodami at full stretch to resist Chatam. A year later the Yorkshire invader cruised home head in chest. Physically he was on excellent terms with himself and when Flashy's Son capsized two out, he only required to keep on his feet to complete the double.

With hindsight Jodami might have been better served by a

harder race. In 1993 his nail biting encounter with Chatam had brought him to Cheltenham running on all cylinders. This time he had enjoyed little more than an exercise canter.

All those who know the horse so well at Foulrice Farm are unanimous that Jodami is a "spring horse." He has run all his best races between the middle of February and the end of April. Like many top equinestars he also enjoys being the centre of attention and the run up to Cheltenham ensures that the latter delight is well satisfied.

Jodami is extremely photogenic so much so that Alec Russell whose pictures are always such a pleasure to peruse is on record as saying that he has only come across two other horses with a similar "look of Eagles". These were Desert Orchid and Red Rum!

When discussing his conformation it is sometimes forgotten that Jimmy Fitzgerald turned down "a first offer" for Jodami on the grounds that his hind legs were too straight and his hocks too curby!

Andy Orkney, the galloping optician turned journalist and commentator, was one of the last to ride Jodami before his second Gold Cup attempt and found him a pleasure to sit on.

He described Jodami as "beautifully balanced with a low head carriage looking where he's going - a dream."

Though naturally anxious about Jodami's virus ridden mid season break, the Beaumonts were satisfied that their champion was in pristine order for the defence of his crown and the knowledgeable crow who scurried for position around the Cheltenham paddock were of the same opinion.

Jodami was rippling with well oiled muscles. His coat shone

with a deep brown lustre and he walked round the crowded parade ring on relaxed spring heels.

Jodami transferred this bon homie to the race course. Always jumping efficiently he travelled smoothly throughout.

Turning for home however, that vital extra gear - so smoothly engaged in 1993 appeared a shade sluggish to operate. Mark Dwyer began to work with more urgency than his admirers had anticipated white Adam Kondrat on his inside was sitting sphinx-like and motionless on The Fellow, who had enjoyed a trouble free passage on the inside and had yet to be put under pressure.

It was 'nip and tuck' to the last but here crucially Jodami fluffed the signals, putting in an extra half stride, brushing through the top of the birch and losing impetus for a vital couple of strides.

Majority opinion holds the view that The Fellow already had the race won at that final fence. I'm not so sure. Had Jodami taken the obstacle in his stride and quickened away up the hill The Fellow would have had a serious battle on his hands and who knows, he might even have been worried out of it near the line.

That alas remains only surmise what is fact is the prospect of another chance for Jodami in March 1995. There is still a lot of mileage on the clock and Jodami will be only ten.

Given a virus free preparation there is no valid reason why 'the eagle' from Brandsby should not be flying high once more when the clock ticks round to 3.30pm on Gold Cup Thursday.

For the record Jodami cost £16,000. After the 1994 Gold Cup had been run his prize money tally stood at £341,338 with plenty more still to come!

Jodami spent the early part of the summer relaxing on John Yeadon's property near Harrogate. He returned to the Beaumonts in mid-July and was reported to have done well out at grass. Jodami was being aimed at the Charlie Hall Chase at Wetherby's end of October meeting. All well being he will then go to Haydock for the Edward Hanmer before travelling south to Kempton for the King George on Boxing Day.

DIZZY

Peter Monteith ended the 1993-94 National Hunt season as Champion Scottish Trainer - always providing that this unofficial contest is decided by the amount of prize money won and not by the number of winners saddled.

Monteith took four horses to Market Rasen on the final day of the season and the £219 gained by Bennan March's fourth place in the Pleasure Prints Novices Handicap Chase was sufficient to tilt the balance in favour of the Rosewell trainer.

His arch rival Len Lungo sent out 27 winners, seven more than Monteith and there is no doubt that Lungo would have clinched the title on both counts had it not been for Dizzy's fighting victory in the County Hurdle at Cheltenham.

The grey was the star performer in Peter Monteith's 25 strong team at Whitebog Farm. She had already repaid over three times her purchase price before she lined up for the County Hurdle and her subsequent neck victory over Diplomatic raised her winnings to £49,560 - not bad for a filly who was claimed for £8,050 after landing a modest claimer on the flat at Edinburgh in the November of 1991.

Dizzy had originally cost 12,500 guineas as a yearling. Closely related to several winners in Germany, she had proved one of the lesser lights in Barry Hills' stable finishing third at Leicester as a Juvenile and prior to her appearance at Musselburgh successful in a small three year old race at

Folkestone.

Lightly framed but workmanlike and very easy on the eye Dizzy had attracted the curiosity of Peter's wily father Colonel William Monteith.

The Colonel has a partiality for grey fillies - especially nicely bred dark coloured greys and his determination as a claimer brooks no argument.

Monteith Junior has been known to question the wisdom of some of his father's purchases but there were no quibbles when Dizzy completed the short journey home to Rosewell.

She was a quality sort at a bargain price and Peter was confident that he was on to a winner from the start.

Dizzy took to hurdling like a duck to water. After two promising outings at Newcastle she opened her account at Edinburgh's early January fixture.

Monteith recalls - "We were probably lucky because Karazan fell when challenging at the last but she was enjoying it and wouldn't have given up without a fight!"

The improvement showed at Musselburgh was maintained next time out at Ayr. Dizzy was beaten four lengths by Good Profile after leading until the second last flight. The winner was rated near the top of the pile as a novice hurdler and Nijmegen who came home ¾ of a length behind Dizzy in third place was no slouch.

Highlight of the filly's first season under rules was her win in the Harcros Scottish Series Championship Final at Ayr in April.

Partnered for the second time by young Tony Dobbin she came from behind to lead at the last and beat Heliopsis by one and a half lengths.

The Colonel was overjoyed and when Dizzy followed up with her fifth success over hurdles at Perth, the Monteiths were well satisfied with their original decision to claim the filly at Edinburgh. Dizzy had also struck up a happy relationship with Tony Dobbin, the young Ulster born claimer, whose ability, now widely appreciated, was at the time a closed book to any one beyond Cumbria and the Borders.

Peter Monteith has always carried out a policy of using up and coming young talent. Liam O'Hara and Michael Moloney have benefitted from his patronage in the past and John Burke of Antonin fame is currently riding winners for the stable.

The anxiety facing Peter Monteith in the run up to the 1992 -93 season was whether the handicapper would inhibit the grey's progress after her splendid campaign as a novice.

The suggestion that Dizzy should continue her career on the flat was discounted. Peter is more than capable of preparing horses to win on the level but both he and Monteith Senior were unanimous that a break out at grass would be the best solution.

Connections were in no doubt that life would be hard for Dizzy second time round, but at the same time she had strengthened up with a further summer on her back.

Ayr's New Year hurdle was her first serious outing and had it not been for Frickley, the Monteiths would have been celebrating Hogmanay with extra hooch.

Frickley, trained by Gordon Richards at Greystoke, was at the climax of a successful run and on level terms he was just too good for Dizzy who had every chance but could not match her rival's turn of foot from the final flight.

It was a salutary lesson - game and genuine though she undoubtedly was, Dizzy was still some way short of top class - shrewd placement would be necessary if the handicapper was to be beaten.

"We knew the mare was fit," said Monteith Junior. "There was a modest handicap hurdle just down the road at Musselburgh, the following week. She would be giving away lumps of weight but the opposition weren't high fliers and the bookies might offer a fair price."

In a big field, Dizzy, ridden this time by Michael Moloney, was sent off at 9/4 with Knights, the mount of Jacqui Oliver second favourite at 6/1.

Edinburgh can present problems. There is always a strong pace and - may, Clerk of the course, Sam Moorshead forgive me for saying so - the bends, particularly the one at the top of the course turning right handed into the back straight, pretty sharp to say the least..

Dizzy was knocked out of her stride on the run to the third but Michael gave her plenty of time to recover and hugging the inside rail on the bottom bend brought her with a well timed run between the final two flights.

Knights meanwhile, flattered only to deceive rushed up to take the lead early in the straight, he had cried enough at the penultimate flight. The lightly weighted Palma's Pride with only 9st 10lbs on his back finished fast but Dizzy was not to be denied. She held on by three quarters of a length much to the chagrin of the layers. (Jinxy Jack was the obstacle to success in the Ship Hotel More Battle Hurdle).

This magnificent looking horse might not quite have had the credentials for the Champion Hurdle, but could murder his rivals at a lower level.

Dizzy's courage was not enough. She did her level best but Jinxy Jack was merciless. He scored by fifteen lengths.

Kelso though was arguably Dizzy's favourite track, she beat Seon by 5 lengths in early March and repeated the success three weeks later leading two out and running on too strongly for Chantry Bartle.

Narrow defeats by Floating River in the Tennant Quaich Hurdle and a valiant attempt to concede thirteen pounds to the firm ground specialist Tapatch at Newcastle ended Dizzy's efforts for the 1992-93 season.

It had been a year of solid progress. The grey could improve marginally in her third season but the objective would have to be major sponsored handicaps; taking on seasoned campaigners off a low weight rather than humping twelve stone on the Border circuit.

Dizzy's physical progress during the three years she was at Whitebog Farm reflected much credit on the part of her sporting trainer.

When she made her first appearance of 1993-94 the mare had developed into a miniature and elegant version of a sherman tank - all quality and muscle. The perfect shape for a hurdler if marginally lacking the scope to tackle fences.

Peter Monteith had pencilled in a spring campaign with the

County Hurdle the stepping stone to the Scottish Champion Hurdle at Ayr.

Dizzy looked round barrelled on her debut at Wetherby in December. Frazer Perratt made sure she enjoyed her reappearance producing the mare with a token challenge four out before allowing her to cruise home in the ruck.

Frazer, incidentally, is one of many committed young jump jockeys who suffer from the current glut of riders. There are too many knocking at the door and only a fraction 'can be let in'.

Frazer's performance has improved dramatically since he has been taken under the wing of Len Lungo and in this capacity his future is assured even if he may never achieve his goal of becoming a top northern rider. Others will not be so lucky.

Dizzy's next race was at Carlisle - a demanding test of a two mile hurdler at the best of times and the grey faced an impossible task under twelve stone. She was ridden by Andy Orkney - his farewell ride as a professional Jockey.

Andy rarely received the credit he deserved. An accomplished and intelligent horseman he suffered from being virtually a freelance but one who had connections with Howard Johnson and John Hellens and was in consequence often passed over by other trainers who believed, wrongly in most cases, that he would be unavailable to ride. Steeplechasing's loss has been racing journalism's gain as Andy has already revealed a natural talent for prose allied of course to an insider's knowledge of the sport.

Andy rode Dizzy from the front. The mare gave him a splendid ride but understandably tired in the closing stages. Reunited with Tony Dobbin, the grey's next two outings resulted in honourable second places behind Home Counties at Doncaster and Grey Power in the Jinxy Jack More Battle Hurdle at Kelso. In each case Dizzy was fighting an uphill battle. Home Counties chose the Doncaster race to produce the sort of form that had once marked him down as a Triumph Hurdle prospect and at Kelso the soft ground proves a decisive advantage for the winner.

By now the Monteiths were beginning to have doubts about the County Hurdle but Tony Dobbin remained buoyant about the prospect of his first ever ride at the Festival.

Dizzy's last race before Cheltenham produced another narrow setback. The mare went down by three quarters of a length to Master of Troy, trained by Colin Parker near Lockerbie and ridden by his younger son David, at the time the season's leading amateur.

The going at Ayr rode soft and the effort of conceding 30lbs to Master of Troy was insuperable.

Dizzy travelled south to Cheltenham more in hope than confidence but her biased supporters remained optimistic.

For the first time in two seasons she would be carrying a light weight and most important of all the ground was good to firm - her favourite conditions. In addition the County Hurdle was traditionally run at a true gallop which would allow Dizzy to lie up with the leaders and maintain her impetus all the way to the line.

The form book indicates that Dizzy was held up behind and made later progress to hit the front close home.

There can be no argument with the later part of this statement but to my way of thinking Tony Dobbin always had his mount lying handy on the inside of the field close behind the leading group. Dizzy appeared to momentarily lose her position running downhill but was staying on strongly approaching the final flight.

Her chances of outright victory were slender crossing the last hurdle but Tony Dobbin persevered and once the mare hit the rising ground she quickened up while those around her began to mark time. Answering her rider's every call. The grey suddenly began to reel in the leaders.

She was eating up the ground as the post loomed into view and with an inspired Dobbin extracting every ounce of effort from his courageous partner the race was won with no more than twenty strides to spare.

Tony said after the race that getting a lead into the final flight had been to his advantage. It gave Dizzy a target at which to aim and ensured that she would not hit the front too early.

For those watching from the stands, that seemed cutting things a bit fine but no-one doubted the brilliance of Dobbins performance in the saddle. It bore all the hallmarks of a future champion jockey. Dizzy was returned at 12/1 though many shrewdies had taken the morning's offer of 25's.

Next stop - the Scottish Champion Hurdle at Ayr. Again the mare was favoured by the sound conditions underfoot, though there were many who felt that the gallant grey might just lack the quality to emulate her Cheltenham triumph.

Corrouge blazed a seemingly invincible trail. He turned into the straight out on his own. Dizzy was the only conceivable danger as the leader crossed the third last.

Tony Dobbin was already in the drive position as the mare stood off the flight and stretched for the crucial long low leap that would gain a couple of lengths in the air.

Flat out she tipped the top bar of the hurdle, turned a half somersault and crashed with a sickening nose dive straight into the yielding turf. The impact broke her neck and the loss of his favourite mare so disturbed Colonel Monteith that he needed hospital treatment to recover.

Dizzy had been a wonderful horse to own. She never failed to give 110% and her fatal fall was the first time that she had hit the ground in her hurdling career.

ANTONIN

The Fellow, the 1994 Cheltenham Gold Cup hero, was sired by Italic and it is not beyond the bounds of possibility that next year's winner will be Antonin, who is also the son of the French bred non-thoroughbred stallion.

Italic first came to the attention of National Hunt enthusiasts through the successes of Rusch de Farges, who was imported to this country by Martin Pipe at the end of the eighties.

The market in French bred saddlebred horses or Selle Francais has received a dramatic boost with the continuing success of household names like Nupsala, Rolling Ball, The Fellow and now of course Antonin.

The common factor about this star quartet is their early maturity. By the time that Italic retired to stud at the age of six he had won numerous races both on the flat and over jumps.

Rusch de Farges landed his first steeplechase at the age of four. When The Fellow won his second King George VI Chase in 1992, he was only seven while Antonin will not reach that mark until next January.

Mental and physical toughness is another characteristic of the French bred jumpers who are frequently the result of a mixed marriage between thorough-bred stallion and a Selle

Francais mare.

In the case of Antonin both his parents come from the non thorough-bred or Autre Que Pur-Sang (other than thorough-bred) category. His dam Pin' Hup is also saddlebred and Antonin's genes dictate that his future on the race course should be specifically restricted to steeplechasing.

The fact that he won a race on the flat before joining Sue Bramall has to be considered a bonus. The knowledge that he proved a dismal failure over hurdles prior to his immediate success over fences should on the other hand be readily accepted.

Antonin is now established as a top British Chaser. He ended 1993-94 with £103,350 in win and place prize money, a total that made him the fifth most successful jumper in training. His achievements helped Sue Bramall to occupy twelfth place in the trainers' table and enabled her to enjoy significantly her best season as a licensed trainer.

Antonin never stopped improving. His victory roll began on New Year's Eve at Newbury with a 25/1 success in the Ladbroke Gold Cup. In late February he romped home ahead of a top class field of chasers to land the Racing Post Chase by six lengths from Docklands Express. At the Cheltenham Festival he gained a bloodless coup in the Ritz Club Handicap chase and had he jumped the Pond fence cleanly might well have ended the season by carrying away the prestigious Whitbread Gold Cup.

Antonin's performance at Sandown proved beyond doubt that the six year old possesses the ability to bridge the gap between leading handicapper and Gold Cup contender. He will not be seven until January and it is reasonable to assume that there is further improvement still to come.

The gelding's dramatic rise to fame has not been a complete surprise to Sue Bramall who has always held him in high regard.

She explains "I'm just so grateful to Anthony Stirk, my vet, for alerting me to the potential market in France. Without his encouragement, I would never have been in a position to find Antonin, let alone buy him."

Stirk, who had previously acted for Michael Dickinson and was therefore fully aware of the french angle, telephoned Sue Bramall out of the blue and asked her to get on a plane and look at some horses for him at the Vichy Sales.

Now a lot of people would have found excuses for staying put but Mrs Bramall not only adores travelling abroad but also has the funds to cover the expenses.

She attended the sales and came home with a couple of horses including the useful handicap chaser Veleda II, whom she purchased only after an amusing exchange with his Gallic owner breeder.

Auctioneers are unnecessary luxuries at most french provincial sales. The vendors parade their wares around the sale, ring and invite private bids from potential buyers.

Sue Bramall recalls, "I made my bid to this fellow and had no intention of increasing the amount. He wanted more so I shook my head vigorously and stalked off to the ladies. I had a feeling that he might be waiting when I came out and sure enough - there he was - rubbing his hands and saying "oui, oui, I sell!"

While she was on that unplanned visit to France, Sue met the

Cypres family, the breeders of the Fellow. Jacques Cypres originally owned Pin' Hup, whom he sold to Pierre Sayet who in turn had the mare covered by Italic with Antonin the end product!

Sue returned to the Vichy area two years later on a buying spree and it was then that she acquired Antonin, who was discovered in a two horse yard outside Nantes. He had already won a provincial flat race in heavy ground and Sue bought him at a bargain price more because of his breeding than his physical appearance.

Antonin is barely 16 hands but he is sturdily built and as events have proved as tough as teak Mrs Bramall initially regarded him as 'plain and a poor mover' but she bought him 'on spec' and passed on a 50% share to estate agent Michael Stanners in whose colours he always runs.

Antonin's first season in this country - 1991-92 coincided with a disastrous campaign for the Bramall horses. The stable was decimated with a viral infection and Sue went the whole season without training a single winner.

Antonin ran six times over hurdles without ever showing a trace of ability - or that's how it seemed. The gelding started at 100/1 on two occasions and the best he could achieve was a remote seventh of 22 behind Tallywagger at Newcastle. It should be noted however, that he was ridden by Joe O'Gorman in five of these races and Joe always recognised his latent promise.

Joe was badly hurt during the spring of 1992 and forced to retire from the saddle. He is now Sue Bramall's Assistant and Head Lad at her Burtree House Stables near Thirsk and in that position has played a major role in Antonin's remarkable renaissance.

His confidence in the French bred gelding must have taken a serious knock the following autumn. Antonin was beaten by an average of 40 lengths in his first two races, was pulled up when tailed off behind Beyond Reason in a 3 mile novice hurdle at Carlisle and then in mid November trailed home seventh of eleven in a bad selling hurdle at Sedgefield.

The transformation was about to take place - even if punters at Ayr on a cold afternoon in January 1993 - had little inkling of its proximity. They allowed Antonin to start at 50/1 in a field of five for his first attempt over fences.

The commentator on that bleak occasion was a certain John Budden and searching through the labyrinth of my memory, I can recall that Antonin tried to run out at 'the horsebox bend' but rallied to regain the lead down the far side and remained at the head of affairs until weakening two out and finishing a tired second to the talented Montpelier Lad.

I was also 'in the box at Edinburgh' a fortnight later when Antonin started a well backed 11/4 chance and led all the way to beat One For The Pot by eight lengths.

I remember congratulating Sue Bramall in the winner's circle and being strangely impressed by her attitude.

"Forget all about his hurdles form. This will be a nailing good chaser. He's bred for it," she said with some emphasis.

Subsequent events have proved how very right both the trainer and her assistant were to hold such views at a time when the name of Antonin was but a gleam of light in the eyes of the shrewdest form student.

Antonin was 'off the blocks'. By the end of April he had run a further five times over fences winning twice at Huntingdon, finishing a creditable runner up to Viking Flagship at Leicester and creating a most favourable impression by gaining a clear-cut success in the Golden Eagle Novices Chase at Ascot.

On this last occasion Antonin made all to thrash Bibendum by seven lengths with horses of the calibre of Snitton Lane and Fighting Words trailing in his wake.

To underline the quality of his performance Antonin then crossed to Ireland to run Viking Flagship to four lengths in the Bank of Ireland, Colliers Novices chase at the Punchestown Festival.

Not surprisingly Antonin's name was included in a variety of 'horses to follow' for the 1993-94 National Hunt Season.

His rapport with Sue Bramall's claiming jockey John Burke was a further factor in his favour. There are few stronger horsemen riding on the northern circuit than John Burke. A Downpatrick lad, he was a contemporary of Tony Dobbin at Jonjo O'Neills stable in Cumbria but did not reveal his true potential until crossing the Pennines and joining Sue Bramall.

Antonin made a steady rather than spectacular start to the 1993-94 season. He injured himself in the horsebox en route to Huntingdon for his reappearance in October - nothing serious but enough to put him out of sorts and he finished fifth. Six weeks later he came up against an in form Clay County at Newcastle and finished second. Four days later he was the only one of six runners to give Young Benz a race at Wetherby and on Boxing Day he would have made Richville pull out all the stops had he not over jumped and failed to get his landing gear down in time when two lengths clear at the third last.

Both Michael Stanners and Sue Bramall, to say nothing of John Burke, are sure that Antonin would have won that race at Kempton but the media's opinion was in direct contrast. The critics felt that Richville was travelling like the winner at the time of Antonin's departure and their conclusions helped towards Antonin's remarkable lack of support before the Ladbroke Gold Cup at Newbury.

Mind you, Antonin could easily have been sunning himself at Cagnes Sur Mer if it hadn't been for the combined opposition of Messrs Burke and O'Gorman.

Mrs Bramall had decided to launch a three pronged attack on the French track. Beauchamp Grace and Able Player were both booked on the ferry but at the last moment Clonroche Driller, the third member of the party, was declared ineligible and Sue Bramall announced her intention of sending Antonin in his place. The shrieks of protest could be heard all the way to Thirsk and the lady relented.

25/1 was a tremendous price for Antonin at Newbury. This, remember was the horse, who had won the Golden Eagle Novices Chase at Ascot and twice given Viking Flagship a hard race the previous spring.

The Cognoscenti declared that Antonin would not stay 3 miles. The Bramall camp begged to differ and there was never any doubt about who was right. Antonin came home alone by twelve lengths.

He was not himself when tailed off behind Zeta's Lad in the Peter Marsh but looked a treat in the paddock before the Racing Post Chase and duly trotted up. Cheltenham proved a formality and the Whitbread only served to underline his toughness and tenacity.

Once again Antonin was turned out in magnificent condition, a picture of health and happiness; his coat gleaming in the spring sunshine and the muscles rippling accross his quarters.

John Burke always had him handy but Antonin fluffed the railway fences on the final circuit and added to his difficulties by blundering badly at the pond fence, the third from home. He dropped back apparently well beaten only to regain his momentum on the run to the final fence.

Antonin was catching Ushers Island hand over fist close home but the post came ten strides too soon and Charlie Swann was not going to be caught unawares.

Antonin had to be content with second place but in defeat he had shown his strength. The stocky little batler will not surrender without a fight. He overcame a series of mistakes to take hold of the bit and fight his way back into contention. He made mistakes at Cheltenham too but shook them off to regain the lead and stride confidently up the hill to convincing victory.

The lessons will have been learnt. Antonin will return in the autumn a stronger and wiser horse.

He could indeed, be a Gold Cup prospect.

For the record, Antonin has won seven times over fences. He has been placed second a further 6 times and has amassed £128,033 in win and place prize money. Not bad for a six year old who cost a fraction of that price to buy out of a two horse yard in central France and was only included in the package because his trainer has an unstunted admiration for the durable qualities of the French bred chaser!

Since running in the Whitbread at Sandown, a 40% share in Antonin has been bought by Paul Venner of Mister Baileys fame, but Sue Bramall and Michael Stanners will retain a major interest.

The horse has summered well and 1994-95 must be an exciting season for all at Burtree House.

LOCHSONG

Jeff Smith's purple and light blue chevron jacket has long held a special place in the Budden wallet. Back in the mists of time when teaching rather than scribbling was one's 'modus operandi,' the early afternoon history period was interrupted by an unexpected call to the telephone.

Simon Raven, the esteemed novelist and long established client of both Victor Chandler and Sunderlands was on the line from Royal Ascot with urgent advice to back an unraced two year old called Chief Singer in the Coventry Stakes.

Time was at a premium with the runners already down at the stalls and the 4th form, (I never reached the dizzy heights of the sixth!) beginning to tire of Richard the Lionheart and The 3rd Crusade.

Rarely has a commission to Corals been dispatched with such summary haste and never has a school bell been heard with more delight.

An headlong dash to the staff room, followed by a frantic twiddling of knobs was rewarded with a memorable lose up of Ray Cochrane, resplendent in that purple and light blue driving an almost black powerhouse of rippling muscle clear of his field with the winning post already within his sights.

Certain colours never lose their appeal and a decade later similar emotions if not alas profit have been irrevocably aroused by the scintillating speed and unquenchable determination of Lochsong.

Timeform's observer at an autumnal Redcar in October 1991 described Lochsong as "a lengthy angular filly, wintry in coat, capable of better" - a neat piece of understatement but undeniably accurate. Within a season Lochsong had won the three hottest sprint handicaps in the calendar and finished runner up to Wolfhound in the Group 3 Diadem Stakes at Ascot.

Rags to Riches would be one way to describe Lochsong's route to fame but the story has all the hallmarks of a pony club potboiler.

Take the filly herself - that appealing combination of knobbly kneed, gawky schoolgirl turned beautiful extrovert princess. Then there is that alluring quality of aloofness and independence of mind that can only be overcome by a mixture of charm, glamour and tender loving care - enter Frankie Dettori, king of the smoothies and finest horseman in the business.

Mix in for 'afters' Jeff Smith, the owner and Ian Balding, the trainer, knights in shining armour, both of them and there are all the ingredients of a fairytale.

The story has yet to run its course. Ideally it will close in triumph with victory in the Breeders Cup Sprint after her second win in the Prx de L'Abbaye. More realistically connections may opt for retirement but whichever fate lies in store for Lochsong, a happy ending is guaranteed. The filly will return to the Littleton Stud, deep in the Hampshire countryside where she was born, has spent all her holidays and where win or lose she is regarded as 'The Queen of Queens'.

While on the subject of studs, let's take a brief look at Lochsong's antecedents.

Were he four footed and hairy Linford Christie would be proud of such forebears...Lochsong's sire Song was a top class sprinter. Her dam, Peekitts Well won five times for Mick Easterby and was herself sired by Lochnager the champion sprinter who numbered the July Cup, the Kings Stand and The Temple stakes aiming his victories as a four year old when also in training at Sheriff Hutton.

Lochsong's grandam Great Grey Niece was the dam of Absolution and her great grandam GreyShoes was closely related to Provideo who won sixteen times as a two year old in 1984. Given such a pedigree Lochsong's preference for five furlongs is hardly surprising though it should be noted that two of her first three races were over seven furlongs and that she scored over that distance in an apprentice riders' event at Newbury.

They say that you should always look at the bride's mother to gleam an accurate ideal of how the future will pan out and Lochsong does appear to have inherited more than a fair share of her mother's characteristics.

Peekitts Well was no beauty as a raw juvenile but she quickly developed into a handsome athlete. She was blessed with plenty of ability, was extremely fast over the minimum trip but acquired ideas of her own and in particular grew steadily more recalcitrant in the starting stalls as her career progressed.

Peekitts Well actually missed the break on her first two outings but was heavily supported to make it third time lucky in a Doncaster maiden event in early May.

Raceform notebook reports that "she caused a few anxious moments in the stalls" but ran home a comfortable winner at 11/10 in the hands-please note-of Willie Carson.

Peekitts Well went on to land competitive nurseries at York and at the Western Meeting at Ayr.

As a three year old the filly won stylishly at Haydock and York but ran down the field when 5/2 favourite to win the steel plate and Sections Victory Cup at the Ascot Heath meeting - a race that Lochnager had won ten years previously under the title of the Bovis Stakes.

The defeat triggered off a steady decline in Peckitts Well's behaviour at the start. She reared up so badly before the beginning the Claude Harrison Memorial at Haydock that she virtually took no part in the race. Later while lining up for the Portland Handicap at Doncaster Alan Amies was moved to write "Peekitts Well was again unruly at the stalls, spent most of her time on her hind legs but still jumped out more or less on terms."

Some would say I dwell too long on the sins of the mother but the sire himself caused problems at the start as he grew older so perhaps one should not be too surprised that Lochsong has appeared to develop similar characteristics this summer.

Lochsong was an ugly duckling as a two year old. She joined Lord John Fitzgerald but when the Newmarket trainer left the country at the end of the 1990 season to take up his present post in Dubai, Lochsong had yet to make her racecourse debut!

Her foreleg joints were the root of the trouble and Jeff Smith had doubts about her future at even the humblest level. He sent her to be trained by Ian Balding with the oft-quoted remark "See if you can win a little race with her if you can."

Jeff has never denied the accuracy of this throw away line so one must accept its authenticity. Ian Balding's horses radiate that 'feel good' factor. On their occasional visits to Beverley, they invariably outshine their rivals in the paddock before humbling then on the course.

No doubt Ian feeds them well but their sleek relaxed outlook must partially reflect the tranquil environment in which they are trained.

Kingsclere boasts some three hundred acres of gallops alone and if a racehorse does not thrive here, he or she is not worthy of the name.

Lochsong has made Kingsclere into her own domain. By all accounts she expects to be treated as the Lady of the Manor and regards "special treatment" as her natural right. Once on the lush turf of her favourite gallops she will release her awesome power but getting there can be another matter.

The transformation from immature ungainly youngster into regal lady has taken less than three years. Lochsong's fragile joints and knees prevented her from making her debut until Salisbury's mid August meeting.

The rich turf of this downland course has long made it a favourite venue for Balding's debutantes and despite the firmish ground Lochsong made a passable first appearance. She raced prominently throughout the seven furlongs and kept on gamely when headed by Miller's Tale at the furlong marker.

Nine month's later Ron Sheather, Racing Manager to the Littleton Stud, revealed that the filly returned to Kingsclere so sore that she couldn't walk freely for another three weeks.

The aim to win that 'little race' was achieved in a modest maiden at Redcar in October. Ridden by Ray Cochrane, Lochsong made all to beat Strimmer by two lengths. It was Jeff Smith's twelfth winner of the season and after the race Ray Gilpin reported in the Racing Post that the filly was likely "to be sent to the sales"!

Lochsong had covered the six furlongs in 1 minute 11.5 seconds. Earlier in the afternoon John Gosden had won the E.B.F. Maiden Stakes with a nicely bred juvenile in a time just four tenths of a second faster. The Gosden winner was called Wolfhound and few if any of those present at the Cleveland course that damp afternoon could have anticipated what stars of the future had passed before their eyes.

Ray Cochrane had intimated at Redcar that Lochsong might have a further race left in her and taking his advice at face value Ian Balding sent the filly to Newbury ten days later to contest an apprentice race over seven furlongs. The trainer was keen to give his talented claimer Francis Arrowsmith every opportunity to widen his race riding experience and Lochsong was both fit and handily weighted.

Young Arrowsmith played his part splendidly, dashing his mount into a clear lead at halfway and holding her together neatly as she began to tie up close home. Lochsong prevailed by a short head and Arrowsmith's horsemanship did not go unnoticed. He was to ride the filly a year later in much more demanding circumstances.

The fact that Francis' name is no longer found among the list of licensed riders reflects the hard nosed combat of modern day racing. Competition for rides has never been more intense. Aspiring Jockeys have to be both physically tough and mentally strong if they are to survive and make the breakthrough into the bit time. "Scully" Arrowsmith remains at Kingsclere as a valued member of the staff.

Lochsong's double success caused Jeff Smith to relent. The filly had begun to mature. She had hinted at a useful turn of foot and equally important she was sure to start 1992 on a favourable mark in the handicap. The figures do not lie yet with hindsight they make remarkable reading. Lochsong started the season on 72 and bowed out in October on a mark of 111 - a rise of 39 pounds with another stone's improvement still to come!

Ian Balding decided to test the temperature in a 6 furlong handicap at Pontefract in April. Francis Arrowsmith had the mount and Lochsong proved that she had trained on by finishing a close up third behind Pharoah Dancer and the evergreen Densben.

The watershed was reached at York in May. Lochsong started 9/2 favourite for the Paul Caddick and Macgay Trophy, a keenly contested six furlong sprint which regularly attracts a large field of experienced campaigners.

Willie Carson was booked to ride. Now memories can be short in racing as much as in any other high profile sport but from the thinly disguised criticism that faced Carson after he had been 'run away' with before this summer's July cup, one could be excused believing that Carson was a hamfisted veteran who hadn't the strength or savoir-faire to keep the country's favourite sprinter on an even keel.

The truth of course is very different. Carson was in no small way responsible for guiding the filly on the path to fame. His enterprising tactics and determined handling ensured that Lochsong put her lenient handicap mark to the best possible advantage and that when Frankie Dettori inherited his position, the mare's confidence was so inflated that steering rather than motivating was the vital quality.

Lochsong won that £12,000 handicap at the Knavesmire. The formbook reads "with leaders going well; led one furlong out driven out." It is worth noting the names of the horses who followed her home. So Rhythmical, Cumbrian Waltzer, Gorinsky and Duplicity occupied the next four places, battle hardened warriors of the northern sprinting circuit and in beating them with such apparent disdain Lochsong had opened up a complete new ball-game.

Ray Gilpin was not surprised to hear that the four year old was to be aimed at the Wokingham. He wrote in the Racing Post the following morning, "Lochsong is at the right end of the handicap and provided she stays sound, there will be other races to be won with her."

Perhaps more significantly Ray quoted Willie Carson's immediate post-race reaction.

Addressing Ian Balding as he entered the winner's circle, Carson asked "Can I partner this one all the time? She's such a lovely ride; so good in fact that she could almost make a jockey redundant!" Nodding in agreement Ian replied "She's very very game and I think we'll stick to six furlongs with her now."

I mention this quote because the myth still prevails that Lochsong is only a "five furlong dasher." At the very highest level, this is arguably true. Lochsong has developed such blistering early speed that she has burnt off her nearest rivals by halfway and maintained her supremacy to the line. This does not mean that Lochsong doesn't stay six furlongs and Jeff Smith's insistence that his mare has this ability to last out the extra furlong is well founded - more effective over the minimum distance yes, but perfectly capable of holding her own over the extra furlong in all but he classiest of brackets.

The handicapper put Lochsong up seven pounds for his York success but it was the draw not the weight that prevented Lochsong adding the Wokingham to his growing list of conquests. The Kingsclere filly was the only horse out of the first eight to have been drawn lower than twenty one. She came out of the number 17 stall, was in front at halfway and plugged on bravely when headed at the furlong marker.

Lochsong continued to defy the handicapper in creating a unique piece of history. She achieved the "impossible" hat-trick of winning, the Stewards Cup, the Portland and the Ayr Cup all in the same season. In each case Lochsong led from pillar to post and her victory at Ayr confounded the majority of the experts and left John McCririck speechless.

To be fair to Channel 4's ebullient mouthpiece, he wasn't alone. Results during the three previous days of the Western Meeting had indicated that low numbers enjoyed an advantage. Lochsong had come out of the hat number 28 of 28. She was steadily rising in the handicap, had shown signs of tiring in the latter stages of the Portland and was now partnered by Francis. Arrowsmith as Willie Carson had been claimed to ride at Newbury.

Lochsong drifted alarmingly before the off at which point "Big Mac" bellowed "One thing's for sure with her draw, Lochsong won't be winning!"

As if spurned by the insult "the lady of the moment" catapulted from the stalls, streaked down the stands rails and spread eagled her rivals to win by 2½ lengths.

To many watchers the thrilling nature of this victory was the most exciting single memory of the entire season. Temporarily it may have silenced John McCririck; more importantly it marked the end of Lochsong's career in handicaps and the start of her challenge for group honours.

Her final race of 1992 was the Group 3 Diadem Stakes at Ascot. Coming only seven days after the Ayr Gold Cup, this was a tall order but reunited with Willie Carson Lochsong fought hard to retain her initial advantage and it was not until inside the final furlong that Wolfhound wore her down. That sixth furlong had begun to be her Achilles heel.

For a while, the step up in class seemed beyond Lochsong. She was beaten in her first four races of 1993; not by much but by sufficient distance to suggest that the bubble might have burst.

Paris House conceded three pounds and beat her two necks in the Palace House Stakes. Lester Piggott attempted to rekindle her winning drive in the Duke of York stakes but to no avail. Frankie Dettori took over for the Temple Stakes but could only keep her head in front until the two furlong marker and Freddie Head faired no better at Chantilly.

A high level conference at Kingsclere led to Lochsong returning home to Littleton for a mid-season break.

Jeff Smith's professional life is taken up with his duties as Chairman and Chief Executive of A.I.M. Group Plc, the public company which is responsible for fitting out and equipping the interior of the world's leading passenger aircraft.

Racing the horses bred at his Hampshire home and planning their future at stud is his all-consuming hobby. Gregarious by nature, he brings a refreshing brand of good humoured optimism to his racing interests; a carefree spirit that appears to have communicated itself to his horses. Lochsong regards the Littleton Stud as "her home from home". She was born there, returns there for the winter and is never happier than when she is cavorting and showing off in her own special paddock.

The unexpected holiday brought a new lease of life to Lochsong. Ian Balding was delighted with the results. The mare arrived back at Kingsclere bigger and keener than ever before. Frankie Dettori took over in the saddle and the partnership flourished. Victory in a listed race at Sandown was followed by all the way success in the King George Stakes at fogbound Goodwood.

The pundits predicted defeat for Lochsong in the Keeneland Nunthorpe Stakes. An eight pound turnaround in the weights with Paris House left the Jack Berry trained grey holding all the aces but Frankie Dettori would not hear of defeat and leaving the stalls at full throttle, Lochsong had her rivals run ragged well before halfway. Paris House tried his hardest to close the gap approaching the final furlong but Lochsong found another gear and won going away by a length and a half.

The emotion of the occasion was all too much for Jeff Smith while a stunned Ian Balding accompanied the delighted Dettori to the weighing room just in case he became so overwhelmed with the excitement of victory that he overlooked the necessity to weigh in.

With the Prix de L' Abbaye Lochsong's ultimate target, Balding opted for the 6 furlong Haydock Park Sprint as final preparation. Wolfhound, energetically ridden by Michael Roberts, and Catrail proved too strong close home but

Lochsong was reserving her acceleration for Longchamp.

It was to be her finest hour. Fast out of the stalls, she set such a fierce gallop that none of her rivals could sustain the pace. Well clear and still hard on the bridle Lochsong showed no signs of stopping. She decimated the opposition to win by a long looking six lengths from Stack Rock with the remainder strung out like washing on the clothes line.

Europe's top sprinter-her election as Racehorse of the Year was but a formality. Yet it had been touch and go midway through the season.

Jeff Smith confirmed later that had she not recaptured her enthusiasm for racing on her return to Kingsclere, she would have been retired to the paddocks. He also revealed the degree of stress that he experienced whenever Lochsong went to post: not because of any personal dread of losing but more because of the public at large being convinced of her invincibility.

Jeff was indeed a proud man in the winner's circle at Longchamp. The original decision to have Lochsong covered before returning to the course this spring was shelved in favour of giving the mare one final season in training.

Until the end of June the plan was working out famously. Lochsong had pulverised her rivals over five furlongs in the Palace House Stakes (a new course record) in the Triple Print Temple stakes from the subsequent Haydock Sprint Trophy heroine Lavinia Fontana and in the King's Stand Stakes at Royal Ascot where she returned to a standing ovation in honour of her five length eclipse of Blyton Lad.

Such has been the extent of Lochsong's superiority that the sporting media who had delighted in their efforts to build her up into a paragon, now turned turtle and searched for possible flaws in her make up.

Defeat in the July Cup led to unwarranted allegations that Lochsong did not stay six furlongs and had yet to beat opposition of real caliber.

Wrong on both counts - Lochsong has proved that she gets the extra furlong; she just happens to be that bit better over the minimum trip.

As for the quality of her rivals, she pulverised Europe's top sprinters in the 1993 Prix de L'Abbaye and at Royal Ascot in the king's stand stalls outclassed Lavinia Fontana, the recent Haydock Park Sprint Cup winner.

Temperament not lack of ability led to Lochsong's disappointing reverse at Newmarket and slavish enforcement of the outmoded parade procedure cost her even more dearly in the Keeneland Nunthorpe Stakes at York.

In between times Lochsong displayed speed and courage of the highest order to win a second King George at Goodwood and if the critics are eager to under value the form of the runner up Mistertopogigo, I would only refer them to the latter's subsequent excellence in both the Nunthorpe at York and the Scarbrough Stakes at Doncaster and finally the Prix de L'Abbaye in October.

Lochsong's two defeats at Newmarket and York can be put down to the common factor of over-excitement in the preliminaries.

As mentioned earlier hereditary characteristics could be coming home to roost, but with hindsight Willie Carson, who appeared to take the brunt of the blame for the filly's "burn up" on the way to the stalls before the July Cup should now be absolved from criticism.

Lochsong grew impatient en route from paddock to course and once set free on the lush green turf simply took charge of her pilot.

Next time out at Goodwood Ian Balding sought and obtained permission from the stewards for Lochsong to go to the stalls early and those who took the trouble to watch were treated to a masterly display of long reined sympathetic horsemanship by Frankie Dettori as he eased the mare down to the start ahead of all distractions.

York was a disaster. The idea of staging a parade before a Group 1 sprint is both impractical and unwise though it has to be said that Jockey Club notes on the subject do seem to give local stewards the power to allow potential troublemakers the opportunity to go down ahead of the field.

Perhaps connections should have pressed the matter more urgently with the officials at the Knavesmire because it is irrefutable that Lochsong's pent up excitement had reached fever pitch long before her turn in the pecking order had arrived.

Defeat was inevitable before Lochsong had been loaded into the stalls though to blame her rider for allowing the mare to race was palpably unfair.

The officials at the start must take this responsibility. They inspected Lochsong and took the view that physically she was fit enough to line up.

Mentally however she was spent and her subsequent performance was inevitable.

Soon after that debacle on the Knavesmire Lochsong was dispatched home to Littleton "to unwind." The mare certainly enjoyed the break and Ian Balding reported that Lochsong had returned to Kingsclere refreshed and ready to fulfill her autumn engagements.

The 1994 Prix de L'Abbaye fully justified his confidence. and she spreadeagled her field for the second year running. She was greeted with rapturous applause by the large British contingent and deservedly so. Lochsong now tackles the Breeders Cup Sprint followed possibly by a fabulously valuable contest in Japan.

Should Lochsong go on to even greater honours abroad, it is not beyond the bounds of possibility that she will stay in training as a 7 year old. In reality, one suspects that she will retire gracefully to prepare for the more sedentary but equally rewarding life as a brood mare.

Jeff Smith might even prefer the second alternative. Describing Lochsong before her second King George Stakes victory at Goodwood he said, "Lochsong never ceases to surprise or astonish. To breed one as good as her once in my lifetime should by my ration but with her you can never know!"

The loss of the stable star will be much harder to take at Kingsclere. In the course of a superbly evocative interview before this year's Nunthope Ian Balding revealed an intimate "behind the scenes" picture of the great mare. He described how she has become to appreciate her status as the public's favourite, loving the attention and preening herself for the constant click of the cameras.

Such is the power of her personality that Chris Scudder, her lad and Seamus O' Gorman and Francis Arrowsmith her work-riders, pamper to her needs with cheerful patience. She apparently takes enormous pleasure in keeping the whole string waiting while she decides whether or not to condescend to take part in early morning exercise. Only royalty can expect such privileges by right but then Lochsong has deservedly gained the title of 'The Sprinting Queen of the Nineties'.